COOKING THE BOOKS
WITH MIKE

Cooking The Books With Mike

Michael Campbell's

Favourite 50 Recipes
For Instant Financial Success

Money Talks
Publishing

Canadian Cataloguing in Publication Data

    Campbell, Michael
    Cooking the Books with Mike:
    Michael Campbell's Favourite 50 Recipes for Instant Financial Success.

    ISBN 0-9683087-0-8
    1. Finance, Personal-Canada. I. Title.

Printed and bound in Canada

Cover design by Chris Dahl, Chris Dahl Design Communications
Editing by Georgina Montgomery, West Coast Editorial Associates
Proofreading by Precision Proofreading, Victoria
Typesetting and production by Axis Interactive Design, Langley
Printing and Binding by Kromar Printing Ltd., Winnipeg

This book is available at special discounts for bulk purchases.
For details, contact High Performance Events,
614-402 West Pender Street, Vancouver, BC V6B 1T6.
Fax: (604) 602-0325 Tel: (604) 602-0395.

To my mother,
Margaret Janet Campbell,
for all her love and support.

TABLE OF CONTENTS

TASTY TAX TREATS YOU CAN'T AFFORD TO MISS

"SELF-EMPLOYED" ENTRÉES

"DON'T DROP DEAD" DANISHES

"MONEY-MAKING" MUNCHIES

"SECURITY" SMORGASBORD

MAKING SENSE OF ABBREVIATIONS

ABOUT THE AUTHOR

LIST OF TABLES

PEOPLE I WANT YOU TO KNOW ABOUT

I'm glad you're reading this section because the people I want to mention made this project a great deal easier. Some of them helped because they owed me a favour. Others helped out of the goodness of their heart, and now I owe them a favour. A few others did it because they wanted to see their name in print on something besides the local police bulletins. I realized that if I thanked them publicly at the beginning of the book, I would save the expense of having to send them an expensive gift. In other words, I'm practising what I preach.

None of these individuals is responsible for any of the shortcomings in the text. On the contrary, their participation contributed greatly to producing a better product than I ever could have on my own.

A big thank you goes to Renée Rosko and Catherine Luckhurst, for always being there when I needed them to tie up loose ends. I want to thank Chris Dahl, the wonderful graphic designer and president of Chris Dahl Design Communications, for his creative flair. I want to thank Georgina Montgomery, of West Coast Editorial Associates, for taking time from her busy schedule to raise the literary level of my work with her editing skills. I asked my accountant, Ken Telford, to read the recipes to make sure I didn't leave out any essential ingredients. My thanks also to Paul Smith for his help with the tables. A big thank you to Deborah Wright, of Precision Proofreading, who ensured the quality control of this book. Richard Deschenes, David Ediger, Michael Cober, and the rest of the Axis Interactive Design team were truly professional during the production of this book.

I want to thank Tom Plasteros and Ian Koennigsfest, of radio station CKNW in Vancouver, for their support and help in making "Money Talks" such an overwhelming ratings success, thereby giving me the opportunity to talk to people across the country about their finances.

I want to thank a group of friends whom I asked to read the text at various stages of development. Their comments went a great way to making sure that the recipes were understandable and easy to follow. My special thanks to Jill Nowak, Kary Taylor, Kevin Konar, Mike Dennison, Nina Parente and Naguib Dhalia.

Finally, I want to thank my wife Cathy and children Courtney, Charlie and Willie for their support and encouragement. ●

ARE YOU ABOUT TO GET FINANCIAL INDIGESTION?

Before I decide if this book is right for you, please take a moment to answer a few questions. Please take your time answering because I really want to get to know you.

Where were you when Paul Henderson scored the final goal in the 1972 Canada vs. Russia series?

Where were you when President John F. Kennedy was shot?

Where were you the night Abraham Lincoln was shot?

If you answered "yes" to any of these questions, then this book is definitely for you. I appreciate that the questions don't seem to have a lot to do with the fact that you're probably throwing thousands of dollars away a year because you don't know the best strategies to maximize your income and minimize your taxes. But I do want you to remember where you were when you picked up this book and started to use some of the recipes – because it will leave just as strong an impression as those other events did. Okay, I'm stretching it a bit.

I could have asked you if you're doing all you can to maximize your income, your investments and your tax savings, but I already knew the answer. There are only two types of Canadians. Those who are too busy to practice the straightforward and legal techniques available to get the most from their money, and those who need to get a life.

While sometimes we love to say we're interested in learning about our finances, our actions reveal a different story. Let me share with you the results of a survey I conducted just two months ago.

QUESTION: Would you rather learn about your personal finances or go skiing or golfing?

RESULT: 93% of the respondents chose the recreational sports. The other 7% said, "Pardon me?"

QUESTION: Would you rather learn about your personal finances or go to a movie?

RESULT: 86% said they would rather go to a movie. Even when they were told the movie starred Emilio Esteves, the number didn't drop. The other 14% asked if the movie was subtitled.

QUESTION: Would you rather learn about your personal finances or take your neighbour's child to a 6:00 a.m. hockey practice on Sunday?

RESULT: 91% said they would rather take the little Gretzky next door to a hockey practice. Even when they were told that Emilio Esteves was the coach, the number didn't drop. The other 9% asked if he were the assistant coach or the head coach.

QUESTION: Would you rather read Tolstoy's "War and Peace" in Russian or learn about your personal finances?

RESULT: 94% asked who Tolstoy was. The other 6% asked if Emilio Esteves was in the book.

I think you're getting the picture. When it comes to our own "to do" list, learning about our personal finances is somewhere between organizing our pocket lint and clipping the toe-nails of our neighbour's pet python. That's why, according to Statistics Canada, 53% of men and 82% of women will need financial assistance from the government, family or friends when they reach retirement age. Fewer than 10% of us will enjoy the same standard of living when we retire, as when we worked.

My own work tells me that 96% of Canadians do not maximize their financial situation. But I also know how you can change that situation and assure your financial prosperity, without altering your lifestyle in any appreciable way. ●

THE MAGIC FORMULA

My goal in writing this book was not to qualify you as a financial planner. I don't want to introduce you to a new hobby and I don't want to prepare you for the Canadian Securities Course. For most of us that wouldn't work. We're too busy with other things, like life.

What I do want to do is introduce you to 50 of my favourite techniques that can have an immediate impact on your personal finances. Too many people do nothing about their finances because they're worried they're missing some important piece of knowledge. They think there is some great big secret out there that only the wealthy know.

Sure, there are some important fundamentals to know that can vastly improve your financial situation, but they really are easy to use and follow. I am convinced that anyone who tries even one or two of the recipes in this book will notice a great improvement in his or her personal situation.

I can't wave a magic wand to put you into financial Nirvana but I can tell you that success with money is not very different from achieving success in any other area of life. It takes commitment and persistence. My suggestion is that you start by making the commitment to follow just one of the recipes from each section initially. Don't change your lifestyle; simply focus on one or two strategies. When you've done that, then add another and on and on.

If you don't think you can follow the recipes because you don't have the money to invest or to make an RRSP contribution, then pay special attention to the sections on saving and taxation. You'll be surprised at how easy it is to find a few extra dollars. You may be even more surprised at the size of the impact those savings can have over time. ●

WHAT YOU REALLY NEED TO KNOW

After reading these recipes you will appreciate the most important fundamentals of creating personal financial success. Wealthy people understand concepts like compound growth, the difference between spending before-tax and after-tax dollars, the future value of a dollar, and the tax benefits of self-employment.

This book concentrates on helping you find money to invest – mainly by introducing you to techniques to reduce your taxes – and then to invest it wisely so that you can create long-term financial security. I could have included a lot more recipes, but that would have defeated my purpose of getting you to focus on a few effective strategies.

My final word of advice is, above all else, take action now. Make time for your finances and you'll be surprised at the incredible difference you can make to your circumstances. ●

"SUPER SAVINGS" SMORGASBORD

"The best thing about money is that it never clashes with anything you're wearing."

– ZSA ZSA GABOR, ACTRESS

THE
"SHOP 'TIL YOU DROP STEW"
SURPRISE

YOU HAVE TO LOVE all those don't throw your money away expressions like "look after the pennies and the dollars will take care of themselves," "a penny saved is a penny earned" and "only schmucks buy retail." (Actually, I think it was my mother who said that.) The fact is, they're true: you can't build a big stack of money if you keep throwing it away. Now, don't get me wrong. Spending money is okay. Throwing it away is not. By simply shifting how and when you buy, you can save enough money to lay the foundation for a valuable investment portfolio.

Think about it. Most of us spend many thousands of dollars a year shopping for everything from groceries to CDs. If we could find a way to save just 20% on the items we purchase, the result would be significant. And the best part is that we would be saving after-tax dollars. One of the most important points to remember about getting a better deal is that you not only save the money on the purchase, you also save the GST and the PST on that portion as well.

Let's say you shopped around, saved $100 on a piece of furniture, and then put that $100 in your wallet. What far too few of us understand is that the real savings are much more than that. In most provinces, the savings on the GST and PST you didn't pay would be at least $14, which would bring you up to $114 in extra money. Now think of it this way. Let's say that if instead of saving the money, you decided to earn enough to end up with that extra $114. The shocking truth is that you (if you're the average Canadian) would first have to earn an extra $193 in income. That's because most of us have to pay about $79 right off the top in income tax. What remains is the $114 you would have needed to purchase the item at full price.

That's why the impact of saving money is so dramatic and ends up being a lot easier to do than getting a raise or a second or third job. I don't know about you, but I think there are a lot more "sale" signs out there than "come on in and let's talk about your raise" memos from the boss. Of course, spending smarter and saving money requires nothing more than using your common sense. The key is to use that sense consistently. ●

TIP
Develop money-saving radar by taking advantage of coupons, in-store specials and entertainment books. If your family purchases $20,000 worth of goods a year, the newly found 20% savings could produce the $4,000 you need for your RRSP contribution. You could then take your tax rebate and pay down a portion of your mortgage or credit card debt. And I promise if you start taking care of things in this way, I'll make you rich.

FACT
A recent survey by Trimark Financial Group found that 23% of the disagreements couples experience are based, at least in part, on financial issues.

THE "SHOP 'TIL YOU DROP STEW" SURPRISE

1. Make a list of all the items you purchase regularly.

2. Plan those purchases. Buy out of season, take advantage of coupons and other price specials, and buy in bulk to take advantage of price breaks. It's easy to save 15% more on most items.

3. Make it a habit to phone at least three sellers for every purchase over $100 in order to compare prices.

4. Plan every purchase over $100 so that you know when these items are most likely to go on sale, and then take advantage of the sale price.

"Whoever said that money can't buy happiness didn't know where to shop."

– GITTEL HUBNICK

WHAT A DOLLAR IN SAVINGS IS REALLY WORTH

If you save a dollar and invest it in your RRSP at 10%, it will be worth over six times more in 20 years. The dollar you save today will be worth $93.05 in 40 years if you invest it at 12%.

WHAT A DOLLAR'S WORTH

$1 INVESTMENT	10 YEARS	20 YEARS	30 YEARS	40 YEARS
@ 10%	$2.59	$6.73	$17.45	$45.26
@ 12%	$3.11	$9.65	$29.96	$93.05

THE "29.5% GUARANTEED RETURN ON YOUR MONEY" OMELETTE

YOU MAY HAVE HEARD the story about former tennis bad boy, Ilie Nastasse. Thieves broke into his hotel while he was playing in a tournament in New York and stole his wife's credit cards. Seven months later, he finally reported them stolen. When asked why he had waited so long to report the theft, Nastasse was quick to explain, "Whoever had the cards was spending less than my wife."

Canadian consumer debt is at record highs, and billions of that debt are sitting on credit cards compounding at 17.5% interest. Of course some cards may be cheaper, but many of those have sign-up and monthly fees. Department store credit cards are significantly more expensive than VISA or MasterCard with monthly compounding rates of 28% plus.

As alarming as these numbers sound, they don't tell the whole ugly story. Credit card interest is paid for with after-tax dollars. In other words, you have to earn a lot more money than the stated interest rate because you first pay tax on your income and then you pay the credit card interest with what's left over.

Think of it this way: If you earn between $29,500 and $60,000 and have interest charges of $1,000, you first have to earn $1,730 and then pay $730 in federal and provincial income tax. What's left over is the $1,000 interest payment. You aren't just paying the 17.5% interest on your credit card – in before-tax dollars you're paying the equivalent of 29.5%.

What really kills me is that some people let their credit card balances run on while they have money sitting in investment vehicles that return as little as 7%. This is a hard concept for some people to get, but the bottom line is that you would have to be guaranteed over 29.5% on your term deposit, Canada Savings Bond or mutual fund to get the same bang for the buck that you would from paying off your credit cards. That's why paying off non-deductible consumer debt is hard to beat if you want to get ahead. ●

TIP

You can enter the elite of personal financial managers by always being aware of the before-tax cost of any purchase. The true geniuses go one step further by figuring out how to make many of their purchases tax deductible. To help you do the same, see the recipes on self-employment.

The
"29.5% Guaranteed Return On Your Money"
Omelette

1. Figure out all the charges that are associated with your credit cards, including the interest rate you pay, sign-up and monthly fees.

2. Find out whether the interest charge is compounded monthly. If it is, the effective interest costs go up dramatically.

3. If you have a savings account, Canada Savings Bonds, term deposits, mutual funds, stocks or any other investments outside your RRSP, sell them to pay off any outstanding consumer loans or credit card debt.

4. If you don't have any other investments to draw from, to pay off your outstanding balances, you must implement a plan as quickly as possible. No matter how difficult it is to discipline yourself to pay down this debt, don't give up until you've succeeded. If you continue to pay 29.5% and more in before-tax interest charges, you'll probably never know financial security in this lifetime.

5. After you pay off your credit cards, do not run up the balance again. If you don't trust yourself, cut up the cards and throw them away.

"A bargain is something you can't use at a price you can't resist."
– FRANKLIN P. JONES

THE "NOT ALL LOANS ARE CREATED EQUAL" OMELETTE

IN THE 1800s, American clergyman Henry Ward Beecher summed up the dangers of borrowing this way: "Interest works night and day, in fair weather and foul. It gnaws at a man's substance with invisible teeth." Actually, just about every great thinker or statesman has warned us against financial indebtedness at some time during their reflections on the human condition. As Victor Hugo put it, "A creditor is worse than a master; for a master owns only your person, a creditor owns your dignity."

Borrowing is simply another way of saying that you are spending tomorrow's income today. The problem is that the cost of the things you're buying grows at the rate of interest you're paying. Worse still is that the interest is compounding, and you're paying with after-tax dollars. Consider this for example: If you purchase a $1,000 item and borrow the money at 10% to pay for it, the cost of the item is rising at the pre-tax rate of 16.5% every year until you pay off the borrowed money. People get into the debt pool and drown, because they don't realize that interest rates on consumer borrowing are quoted in after-tax dollars, but for the average Canadian the effective rate is at least 40% higher in pre-tax dollars.

That's why, if you don't have the cash to pay down your highest interest rate debt, then consider switching it with lower cost loans. Department store credit cards usually have rates around 29%; regular credit cards average 17%. Compare that with mortgage debit of 7% or RRSP loans at 5%. The savings from making the switch from high to low interest rate loans can be substantial.

If your mortgage is coming due, you may want to consider adding the balance of your credit cards or other consumer loans to your mortgage and then paying them off with the lower rate mortgage money. Or if you have money put aside to make an RRSP contribution, you would be better off taking that money and paying off your credit cards and then borrowing for your RRSP. For example, if you had $5,000 earmarked for your RRSP contribution and instead paid off your credit card, you'd save $850 in interest charges. If you borrowed $5,000 for your RRSP the total interest charges would be less than $250. This simple switch would save you $600 in interest charges. ●

TIP

If you're switching credit card debt for mortgage debt, be sure that you make extra principal payments on your mortgage to pay off that extra debt. You do not want to carry that credit card debt for the life of your mortgage. And after you have made the switch, it is essential that you do not run up your credit card debt again.

WARNING

The accounting firm of Deloitte & Touche has issued a series of "warning signals" to help you determine if you are in a debt crisis. Here they are: you use credit to create income; you stall one creditor to pay another; you have no money before pay day; you charge more than you pay on account; you don't know your real monthly expenses; or you have no savings.

THE
"NOT ALL LOANS ARE CREATED EQUAL"
OMELETTE

1. Make a list of all your debts, including credit cards, consumer loans and mortgage.

2. Review the interest rates, frequency of payments and compounding features of those debts.

3. If your mortgage is coming up for renewal, check with your mortgage officer about increasing the size of your borrowing to pay off your credit card or other high-interest rate debt.

4. Alternatively, if you were planning to use money on hand to make your RRSP contribution, consider instead taking advantage of extremely low RRSP loan rates to borrow for your plan. Use the money you had on hand to pay down high-interest rate debt.

5. Use any tax refund from your RRSP contribution to pay down your highest outstanding interest rate debt.

"If it isn't the sheriff, it's the finance company. I've got more attachments on me than a vacuum cleaner."

– JOHN BARRYMORE, ACTOR

"SECOND-HAND" SOUP

STANDING IN FRONT of a class of graduating high school seniors a couple of years ago, I realized, 20 minutes into my talk about the importance of financial planning, that there was a real danger of most of the class lapsing into a deep coma. I started to sweat. Fortunately, a young lady (who looked like she had been beaten up and dressed by Madonna) blurted out, "That's all fine, but what are the easiest ways to get enough money to buy all the CDs you want?" Rising to the challenge, I shot back the two strategies that immediately came to mind: "You could follow what I call, 'The Gabor Gambit,' (after the Gabor sisters) and marry rich; or you could try, 'The Kennedy Classic' and inherit money." She thought that this was great advice, and immediately declared she was going to think about dumping her boyfriend and putting herself up for adoption.

But that wasn't all she wanted to know. She wondered whether there was anything else she could do to impact her finances immediately. I said that while the advice I was about to offer didn't sound particularly dramatic, an effective way to stretch her dollars and increase her savings was to let someone else pay for the depreciation of the item. She looked puzzled, so I added, "It's just another way of saying, 'Buy your CDs second-hand'."

It may not sound earth-shattering to suggest that you shop second-hand, but in fact most people don't understand just how large an impact it can have on your finances.

I can't emphasize enough the value of saving a dollar when you measure it over time. For example, if you could save $50 a month by buying a couple of items second-hand, and you then invested that money in your RRSP at 10%, in 40 years you'd have $280,000.

The impact is even more dramatic when you're buying a big-ticket item, such as a $20,000 car. You could save as much as $3,000 on a one-year-old car that is basically as good as new, and you'd pay less tax because the purchase price has been reduced. (If you buy the car in a private sale, you'd avoid paying the GST altogether.) The savings are further compounded if you're having to borrow money for the purchase. By avoiding having to finance the extra $3,000, for example, you could save up to $200 a year – or $1,000 over the life of a five-year loan. But I'm not stopping there. Let's say you're 36 years old and you put that $3,000 savings into an RRSP, compounding at 10%, until your retirement at 65, you could end up with as much as $60,000. Not a bad reward for buying second-hand. ●

TIP

Understanding that the value of a dollar grows dramatically over time when invested is a key to financial success. For example, if you save $100 every year, starting at age 25, and invest it in an RRSP at 10% until your retirement at 65, you will have $48,685.

"SECOND-HAND" SOUP

1. Make a list of items you need or desire that are appropriate to buy second-hand. Consider, for instance, children's sports equipment, furniture, home renovation items, videos and cars.

2. Make a habit of comparing the cost of buying new with the cost of buying second-hand goods.

3. Go to garage sales, demolition sales and consignment stores to find the best bargains. Check local classified ads and newspapers that specialize in private sales.

4. Make it a goal to save at least $50 a month by buying second-hand.

5. Take the money you saved and make an RRSP contribution. You will get a tax refund and a growing nest egg.

"I had plastic surgery last week. I cut up my credit cards."

– HENNY YOUNGMAN

"SLOW DEATH" STRUDEL

I REMEMBER SEEING a multiple-choice question a few years ago that summed up the essence of the 1980s. It went something like this:

What was the biggest lie of the '80s?

a) I only read it for the articles

b) my BMW is fully paid for

c) I don't usually do things like this with a stranger

The answer is c), my BMW is fully paid for. Now that's what I call fiction. And it's more popular than ever.

With the prices of new cars rising, leasing has become even more popular today than it was in the '80s. The only problem is that when you lease a car, it's a lot more like renting than it is making payments to own. That's why lease payments are generally lower than making monthly loan payments to buy a car. At the end of the loan payment period, you own the car. At the end of the lease period, you still have to make a significant lump sum payment.

Let me give you an example. Let's say you leased a new $20,000 car for 48 months. Your monthly payments would probably be $359. At the end of the lease you could buy the car for $8,000. Your total cost would be 48 months times $359 plus the lump sum of $8,000 – a total of $25,232 (plus taxes.) You may also add to your total cost by driving over the allowable mileage limit. Most leases carry a mileage restriction over the life of the lease, and when that limit is breached there is an extra per-kilometre cost.

If, instead, you borrowed the full $20,000 to buy the car at 7% from a financial institution, your monthly payment would now be $478. At the end of four years you would own the car outright for a total cost of $22,943 (plus taxes.) In other words, it would cost you $2,400 less than having leased the same car.

As expensive as leasing may be, if the car is used for business you can write off more of the monthly payments with a lease than you can with your monthly car loan payments. The whole monthly lease payment is tax deductible to a maximum of $550 a month. In the case of a car loan, only the interest cost and depreciation of the vehicle are deductible. The result is that you can deduct more from your income by leasing, but that is partly because leasing is more expensive. ●

TIP

The leasing concept is now becoming popular for people buying home appliances. Beware: rent-to-own payment schemes are extremely expensive. It is much better to borrow the money from a financial institution than to rent-to-own or to use a department store credit card, or MasterCard.

FACT

A $680 colour TV costs $1,775 when total costs of the typical rent-to-own plan over a 24-month period are added up. That compares to $862.49 to purchase the same TV using a department store credit card, or $795.41 using MasterCard.

"SLOW DEATH" STRUDEL

1. When buying a new car, go to your financial institution to get preapproved for a loan. The shorter you can afford to make the term of the loan, the less interest you will pay and hence the less overall cost of the car.

2. If you are comparing lease costs between dealers, make sure you find the size of the lump sum (residual value of the car) you have to pay to purchase the car at the end of the lease. Ask for a written list of all fees associated with the lease, including any down-payment costs.

3. Ask if there are any mileage restrictions and if there are, what costs might be incurred for going over the limit. In addition, ask if there is a required maintenance schedule.

4. When seeing your banker for a loan, don't be afraid to ask him or her to do a comparison of the costs between leasing and borrowing. There are several computer programs available to help you do the calculations. A financial planner or accountant would also be able to do the number crunching for you.

"If you think nobody cares if you're alive,
try missing a couple of car payments."

– EARL WILSON, NEWSPAPER COLUMNIST

RETURN ON TERM DEPOSIT NEEDED TO EQUAL PAYING DOWN YOUR LOAN

YOUR LOAN	APPROXIMATE MARGINAL TAX RATE	
RATE %	40%	50%
8.0	13.3	16.0
10.0	16.7	20.0
12.0	20.0	24.0
14.0	23.3	28.0
16.0	26.7	32.0
28.8	48.0	57.6

In other words, if you are in a 40% marginal tax-bracket, you would need to get a return of 13.3% on your term deposit to equal the benefit of paying off your 8% consumer loan.

"Car Saving" Casserole

SIX HUNDRED THIRTY-FIVE thousand, two hundred, twenty-two. That's how many songs I counted that have been written about cars. And that doesn't include songs like the Beach Boys' *I Get Around* or Bruce Springsteen's *Thunder Road*. The number would be a lot higher if I counted every song that mentioned cars. The point is that we love our cars. We love them more than our environment, our personal safety and our financial well-being.

That's why any suggestion to leave them in the garage is apt to meet with a great deal of resistance. There's a big list of things people are willing to sacrifice before they'll let go of their wheels but the fact remains that cars are incredibly expensive to own and operate. The Canadian Automobile Association states that the average cost of running a car is 35.9 cents a kilometer. According to numerous consumer publications, the average yearly cost of driving is between $6,000 to $8,000 per year.

Think about it. You pay insurance costs, parking, gasoline and maintenance as well as depreciation on the vehicles as the resell value drops every year. And if you are like me, you can add in the cost of a few parking tickets and the odd driving-related fine. The good news is that if you are self-employed or earn commission income, you can write off those car expenses which are incurred to earn income. The rules governing what and how much is deductible are complex and you should ask an accountant for some help.

My point is much more straightforward. You should consider if you can afford to get along without a car. If you are part of a two-car family you should really give the idea of eliminating one some serious thought. The savings can be massive when measured over several years. And the impact of those savings can be greatly magnified when invested properly. The *Financial Post's* Jonathan Chevreau estimated that if he ditched his car for commuter rail, the annual savings could be $4,300. Do that for 40 years and you'd have $171,744. If you had invested that money every year in an RRSP and received an annual growth rate of 10%, you would have ended up with $2,093,463 in the plan. You also would have got a tax refund of about $2,000 per year which would be enough to pay for all your public transportation and a few cabs to boot.

The decision to own and operate a car is obviously yours. I want to make sure that you understand how expensive it is. ●

TIP

One way to save a few dollars on your insurance costs is to arrange for your car insurance to expire on the day your longest holiday of the year starts. That way you don't have to renew it until you are back. In other words, if every year you take the first two weeks of July off, then have your insurance expire on June 30th. If you are taking a two-week holiday, you don't have to renew it until July 15th and you therefore save about 10% off the cost of your insurance. A great many two-car families should be doing this strategy if the family regularly goes away for the summer and you could do without one of the cars for that time period. The overall savings will be in the hundreds of dollars.

"CAR SAVING" CASSEROLE

1. Consider selling your car and taking public transit and taxi cabs instead.

2. If you are not sure if this strategy is for you, the next time your car insurance has to be renewed, delay it for a week and experiment with a combination of public transit, car pooling and taxi cabs. At the very least, you will end up saving one week's worth of insurance costs and gasoline.

3. If you choose not to sell your car, you should then consider leaving it at home half the time. The savings could be as much as $2,500 a year.

4. My suggestion is to take any savings and make an RRSP contribution. Then take your tax refund, spend half on paying for your alternative methods of transportation and the other half on rewarding yourself.

"Never lend your car to anyone to whom you have given birth."

– ERMA BOMBECK, AUTHOR

"FIVE POINT SAVING" FILLET

DO YOU REMEMBER "The Partridge Family" on TV? Well, Shirley Partridge could teach most of us a thing or two about making ends meet. Shirley used to say, "There are as many ways to save money as there are to spend it." And she would know. She was a widow with four mouths to feed and no noticeable skills or talent – which is why she had to turn to miming songs for a living. So don't try and tell me you can't save enough to invest: even Shirley managed to save enough for a bus, and the rest is music history.

The key to saving is to review your spending habits and check whether there are some painless ways to save some money and put it to better use. Shirley had the right idea when she set herself a realistic monthly goal and created a special savings account to help her keep track. I'm sure you can think of your own ways to save, but here are a few ideas that Shirley and her family used to get her started in the right direction.

1) She stopped buying lottery tickets. Shirley found out that she was more likely to get struck by lightning twice than win the lottery. According to Stats Canada, the average family spends in the neighborhood of $200 a year on lottery tickets. Shirley used that $200 instead to make an RRSP contribution and immediately received a tax refund of $80.

2) Shirley, Danny and Keith quit smoking. There is nothing more boring than a born-again non-smoker, but kicking the habit can save a ton of money. If many of us did nothing more financially prudent than investing the savings from not smoking, we would still manage to build a huge nest egg by the time we retired.

3) Laurie saved a fortune by not using bank machines at other financial institutions than her own. Transaction costs were ridiculously high. She also found that by planning her withdrawals from both the cash machines and her chequing account, she could save over $125 a year in service charges.

4) When Shirley finally had the money for the family bus, she saved hundreds of dollars by shopping around for insurance. She also raised the collision deductible to $500 from $100 and added to her savings. As well, she shopped around for insurance for her 1997 Honda Accord and saved an additional $117.

5) When Shirley finally had enough money together to invest, she shopped around for the best interest rates and commission structure.

Shirley had a ton of great ideas, but what she really did well was just get started. By choosing a savings goal and focusing on it, she was amazed at how fast the money added up. ●

TIP

Don't be afraid to become an expert on money-saving techniques. There are numerous publications to help you, including books like "The Best of Cheepskate Monthly" and "Penny Pinching."

"FIVE POINT SAVING" FILLET

1. Set a monthly savings goal. Be sure to make it attainable. The key is to change your spending habits, not your standard of living.

2. Set up a separate bank account to put your savings in. Every time you know you saved money, put that amount in the special account to help you keep score.

3. Ask your friends or family for their favourite money-saving ideas and then see if you can put them into practice.

4. Stop buying lottery tickets or gambling. The odds are stacked against you and you would be much better off making an RRSP contribution and getting a sure-fire return on your money. With an RRSP contribution, you're guaranteed an instant win with your tax refund.

5. If you smoke, do your best to quit, by joining a program if necessary. Invest all the money you start to save by not smoking.

6. If you use bank machines, reduce your service charges by making fewer withdrawals. Never use bank machines from financial institutions other than your own, because the extra charges are far too high.

7. Shop around for private car insurance. You could save hundreds of dollars by using the phone for a few minutes to compare prices. Raise your collision deductible to $500, maybe even to $1,000. Chances are if you have an accident that requires repairs for less than that amount you wouldn't claim it anyway because of the rise in your premiums that would take place.

$50 PER MONTH SAVINGS COMPOUNDED AT 10% PER YEAR TO AGE 65

One of the biggest lessons of successful personal financial management is – don't procrastinate. Look at how much money it costs just to wait a single year to start saving and investing. Use the savings techniques and invest your rewards.

Begin Savings at	Total at age 65	Cost to Wait
age 25	$292,111	
age 26	$264,955	$27,156
age 30	$178,876	$113,234

"TERM INSURANCE" TORTILLAS

ONE OF THE UGLIEST scenes I ever witnessed at an investment conference took place a few years ago in Kelowna. A very well-known investment commentator stood up in front of 500 people and told them that in all probability they had the wrong insurance and, what's more, had overpaid for it. Not surprisingly, the insurance people in the audience were not impressed, although I thought they overreacted when they brought out the tar and feathers.

The only problem is that the commentator may have been right. Far too many people are overpaying for the wrong kind of insurance and it's costing them thousands of dollars. At the risk of oversimplifying and getting tarred and feathered myself, let me explain. I definitely believe that if you have dependents you need insurance. As a rule of thumb, you should have enough coverage to equal 5 to 10 times your current annual income. If you don't have any dependents, then you should save your insurance money and invest it elsewhere.

Now here's the difficult part. Which kind of insurance do you need? Most financial advisors agree that the best value is term insurance, not whole life insurance. Term insurance is straightforward. You pay a monthly amount and, if you die, your beneficiaries receive a fixed amount of cash. Whole life insurance, on the other hand, promises to pay a fixed amount when you die, but it also has a cash value if you terminate the policy.

Some people prefer the idea of whole life simply because if they don't die (in the short term anyway), they still get some money in return. I think they're actually disappointed that they don't get to collect the whole amount, but their feeling is that at least they get something for all those premiums paid. What they don't realize is that they are paying higher premiums for the ability to cash in the policy. It's the magic of long-term compound interest that makes the cash in value seem so attractive. Most experts agree that you would be better off taking that extra you have to pay in premiums for whole life and using it instead to purchase term insurance, pay lower premiums, and invest the difference directly in mutual funds.

The insurance business has seen an explosion in the number of products available in the last few years, so it is even more confusing for the consumer than ever. The one rule to remember, however, is: Buy insurance for its intended purpose of protecting your dependents financially if you die. Don't use it as a savings or investment account. ●

TIP

Keep your term insurance to 5- or 10-year increments. (Longer terms cost more and provide no more coverage.) Shorter terms force you to review your situation from time to time to see if your policy needs adjusting. Save more money by passing up riders like accidental death. You should have proper coverage whether you die by accident or not. Do purchase renewable insurance, however, because it allows you to renew at the end of the term no matter what has happened to your personal situation.

"TERM INSURANCE" TORTILLAS

1. Make a list of those people who are financially dependent on you. You do not need insurance if you have no dependents. You also do not need insurance for children. You are better to cancel such policies and invest the money you were paying in premiums.

2. Determine the amount of yearly income you and your dependents would need to maintain their current lifestyle.

3. Check to see if you have any insurance coverage through your employer and determine how much would be paid out upon your death. Many companies cover their employees through a group plan. If you find you do have coverage, ensure the correct beneficiary is identified on the policy.

4. Make sure the combination of your insurance policies provides coverage to at least 10 times your annual net salary. In addition, your coverage should pay enough to cover outstanding debts.

5. Shop around for any insurance needs you might have outside the group plan your employer provides. Make sure the policy you buy is automatically renewable and non-participating.

"The difference between sex and death is that with death you can do it alone and no one is going to make fun of you."

– WOODY ALLEN, DIRECTOR AND COMEDIAN.

THERE'S NOTHING LIKE
A LITTLE HOME BAKING

*"Never get deeply in debt to someone who cried
at the end of Scarface."*

– ROBERT S. WEIDER

"SHORTEN UP AND FLY RIGHT" FONDUE

IT'S A CLASSIC good news, bad news story. The good news: there are about a half dozen strategies available to us to reduce the total cost of our home mortgage. The bad news: the majority of us don't use them and it's costing us dearly. No wonder we don't have as much money in our pockets as we should.

This is one strategy that I can't believe everyone doesn't use. It's easy, doesn't cost much and can save you a pile of money.

It must be habit, but the majority of us still take out a mortgage with a 25-year amortization period. By changing the period to 20 years instead, you can save tens of thousands of dollars in interest charges and it costs so little to do it. Let me give you an example. Do you know Andy Sipowitz, the gritty detective on TV's "NYPD Blue"? In the program's second season, Andy was falling in love with the District Attorney. He decides to move out of his bachelor dump and into a nice two-bedroom apartment in Queens in an effort to impress her. He also decides to take his mortgage with him. He has a $100,000 mortgage amortized over 25 years at 7%, and his monthly payment is $700. Over the life of the mortgage, Andy would end up paying $110,122 in interest alone.

Before Andy signs the final transfer, he happens to tell Lieutenant Fancy about his plans. Fancy gets agitated and insists that Andy change his amortization period from 25 to 20 years. Just to get him off his back, Andy decided to look into it.

He finds out that his monthly payment would rise to $769, but his total interest cost would drop to $84,631. On his salary, Andy knows he can afford the extra $69 – and he knows even better he can't resist the $25,491 in interest savings over the life of the mortgage. After all, the savings represent nearly a year's after-tax salary. The other bonus is that the apartment becomes his outright five years earlier. Naturally,

Andy buys the two-bedroom, shortens his mortgage amortization period and marries the District Attorney. ●

TIP

Because mortgage payments are made with after-tax dollars, that means that every dollar of interest saved is really the equivalent of earning as much as double that in salary (depending on your marginal tax bracket.)

"SHORTEN UP AND FLY RIGHT" FONDUE

1. Make sure you know all the terms and conditions associated with your existing mortgage. Know the number of years over which you're amortizing the mortgage.

2. Ask your financial institution for the monthly cost if you were to shorten the amortization period by five years. If you can afford the increase in monthly costs, make the switch.

3. If there's a small administration fee to shorten the amortization period, ask your financial institution to waive it because you're a good customer.

4. Keep in mind that it doesn't really matter what your financial institution's attitude is to making the switch. Virtually all mortgages allow the owner to make extra principal payments on a regular basis, which is what you're actually doing.

"I'm absolutely ecstatic. My agent just phoned me and told me they discovered land on my property in Florida."

– JACK BENNY

THE "$55,000 MORTGAGE SAVINGS" SURPRISE

YOU MAY BE ONE of those Canadians who take a great deal of pride when our financial institutions announce record profits. Perhaps a little smile crosses your face as you ponder the possibility that your mismanagement of your mortgage terms was probably what put your favourite lender over the top.

But enough is enough. By making one simple change to your mortgage payment schedule, you can save literally tens of thousands of dollars in mortgage interest payments. It's as straightforward as making your mortgage payments bi-weekly instead of monthly. Yes, it will cost you a little more in the short term, but the interest savings are significantly higher over the term of the mortgage.

Consider this example. Let's say you have a $150,000 five-year mortgage at 8%, with a 25-year amortization. Your monthly payments would be about $1,145. The sobering part is that over the life of that mortgage you'll pay a whopping $193,438 in interest alone. Now, instead, take that mortgage payment, divide it in half and pay it every two weeks instead of monthly. Your payment is now $572 bi-weekly. The result of this little change means that at the end of 48 weeks, you have made the equivalent of 12 monthly payments, and the extra two bi-weekly payments every year will go to paying down the principal. The resulting savings are incredible. First of all, your mortgage will be paid in full in only 18 years instead of 25. Second, you'll save a grand total of $58,736 in interest.

If you still need convincing, think how much you'd have to earn to end up with $58,736 extra after-tax dollars to spend or invest. (Remember mortgage payments are made with after-tax dollars.) If you're in a 40% marginal tax bracket, you'd need an additional $99,528 in income to end up with that kind of savings in your pocket. ●

FACT

Industry insiders estimate that over 45% of mortgage holders in Canada have chosen the most expensive terms available for their mortgages.

THE "$55,000 MORTGAGE SAVINGS" SURPRISE

1. Go to the financial institution that holds your mortgage and tell your lender you want to switch your full monthly payments to bi-weekly. Make sure your bi-weekly payments are at least half of your former monthly payments.

2. Ask about the cost of making this change. It typically ranges from no charge to a one-time administration fee of about $50. If you do the majority of your banking with the one institution, ask that any fee be waived.

3. This one is so easy to do. I want you to put the book down and phone your mortgage lender immediately.

"When you combine ignorance and borrowed money, the consequences can be interesting."

– WARREN BUFFET

"HALF POINTE" PRALINE

HAVE YOU NOTICED that the same person who is willing to nit-pick over the smallest of details when it comes to things you do would never dream of negotiating for a better price with a total stranger in a store? I'm talking about your spouse or significant other. You know, the person who wants a separation just because you leave the cap off the toothpaste or greet the dog more enthusiastically than you do him or her. When it comes to trying to make a better financial deal with a sales person, however, your mate probably wouldn't think of it. Why torture a stranger when there's someone to hassle at home?

Let's leave the family alone and hassle the bank! I'm talking about shaving a little off your mortgage rate. When it comes to our mortgages, far too many of us accept the posted mortgage rate as if it were recently handed down by Moses. In fact, these rates are not written in stone, and negotiating a lower rate can save you thousands of dollars. In today's competitive environment, it's even expected that you'll do it. For most of us, I'll bet it's the most money we'll ever save in the shortest amount of time.

Let me give you a little-known historical example from the world of TV. When Bonanza's Lorne Greene first saw the Ponderosa, he immediately fell in love with it and decided he'd do anything to live there. The half-million acre plus spread was on the market for $237,000 (remember this was a few years ago.) Lorne only had

$37,000 saved up, so he had to get a mortgage for the rest. The bank's five-year rate was posted at 7%. Lorne knew that would be a stretch because his monthly payments would be about $1,402. On the advice of his son, Hoss, Lorne went to the bank and promised to bring all his business there if the manager would take a half point off the posted mortgage rate. The manager, realizing that he could have a long-term relationship with all the family, agreed on the condition that Lorne change his name to Ben Cartright. Lorne thought that was a bit peculiar, but agreed. His savings amounted to $62 a month or $18,600 over the life of the mortgage. As you'd expect in TV, everyone lived happily ever after. ●

TIP

When you are thinking of getting into the home market for the first time, you'd be wise to get a preapproved mortgage. The norm is to get a rate guarantee for 60 days. If, at the end of that period, you still do not have a home to buy, then get approved for another 60 days. And don't worry if the rates go up, because you are guaranteed the lower rate; and, if they go down, you get the benefit of the drop. When it comes time to negotiate a mortgage or a house price, you'll find that having the financing in place is a big advantage.

"HALF POINTE" PRALINE

1. Look in the newspaper for a listing of the posted mortgage rates. Identify the lowest rates and the financial institutions offering them.

2. Go to your existing financial institution and tell whomever you deal with that you want a half point off the posted rate for your renewal or new mortgage. Say that, in return you're prepared to move all your personal banking there, including RRSPs, chequing account and so on.

3. If your financial institution agrees, you have no problem. If it doesn't, take your business elsewhere and be prepared to negotiate again.

4. Depending on the extent and size of the business you can bring with you to a financial institution, you may be able to negotiate other perks like a free legal package, property appraisal and mortgage application fee.

5. Keep in mind that the more equity you have in the home, the more likely you are to get a better rate because the bank's risk of not being able to recover the mortgage money is negligible. You are in the driver's seat: financial institutions are in a highly competitive market today, so make yours work for your business. If it isn't treating you like a valued customer, find one that will.

"I have enough money to last me the rest of my life, unless I buy something."

– JACKIE MASON, COMEDIAN

"DOUBLE-UP" DREAM CAKE

YOU MAY REMEMBER that when billionaire Howard Hughes was getting on in years, he spent a great deal of time living in the penthouse of the Bayshore Inn in Vancouver. Years later, I bumped into a middle-aged woman who claimed to be working as a chambermaid at the Bayshore during that time. I asked her if she had any stories to tell about the experience. She said the one she remembers most clearly was the time Howard was pontificating to his staff on the keys to financial security. Of course, I wanted to know more. According to the maid, when Howard was a young man and full of debt, he had a simple rule to follow. He appreciated that compound growth of his debt was a dangerous game, especially when the interest costs on that debt were paid with after-tax dollars.

His solution was to practice one simple discipline. At the beginning of the year, he would double-up his first mortgage payment. He understood that doing it was the equivalent of getting an investment return of about twice his mortgage rate, and that those savings would compound for the entire life of his mortgage. Howard also knew that there were very few better places to put his money. (By the way, the rumor is that Bill Gates is using the same strategy to pay down the mortgage on his $53 million [US] home in Washington State.)

Let me give an example of the kinds of savings we're talking about. If you had a $100,000 mortgage, with a standard 25-year mortgage and a 7% interest rate, your monthly payments would be $700. The total interest costs would be $110,122 over the life of the mortgage. Now, by simply doubling-up the first payment each year to $1,400, your total interest cost would be only $86,642. For an extra $700 a year invested in your house, you can save $23,480 in interest costs and pay off the house in just under 21 years instead of the 25 you signed up for. ●

TIP

If you combined a couple of the mortgage strategies outlined in this book, the savings would be even greater. For instance, if you shortened the amortization period to 20 years on your $100,000 mortgage (paid monthly at 7%) and then doubled the first payment of every year, your total interest cost would be $69,418. That's a savings of $40,694 after-tax dollars.

"DOUBLE-UP" DREAM CAKE

1. Phone your financial institution and ask if your mortgage allows you to double-up at least one payment per year. This shouldn't be a problem, as virtually every mortgage allows a lump sum payment on the yearly anniversary of its being taken out.

2. Multiply your normal monthly payment by two and then put that additional money in as soon as possible. From that point on, do the same thing every year. You are not obligated to put down a lump sum every year. It simply makes good financial sense.

3. There should be no other costs associated with making this lump sum payment. If you feel you can afford to double-up your payments more than once a year, do it. The interest savings will simply multiply.

"The fellow who owns his own home is always just coming out of a hardware store."

– FRANK HUBBARD, HUMOURIST

GRANNY'S "FAVOURITE TAX SAVINGS & MORTGAGE HELPER" MERINGUE

AMERICAN WRITER AMBROSE BIERCE once defined an acquaintance as being someone we know well enough to borrow from but not well enough to lend to. If that's the case, let's hope that you have a few acquaintances who consider the fact that you're related by blood to be significant. Actually the strategy will work with anyone willing to give you a large sum of money.

The idea is to shave a point or two off your mortgage while creating some tax-free income for someone you care for. Many people call this a "granny mortgage" which is probably because grandmothers may be the only ones in your family with sufficient cash and a warm enough heart to give you $100,000 for your mortgage. Now, the operative word here is "give," because there are no tax consequences to giving money to any adult other than your spouse. In other words, the $100,000 would be tax free. This may date me, but do you remember John Barrisford Tipton? He's the guy who gave away a cashier's cheque for $1,000,000,000 to complete strangers every week on TV in the early 1960s, but the important point is that none of them ever paid tax on it.

The next step is to reciprocate the wonderful generosity of your grandmother (or whomever is your benefactor) by giving her some money in return. You could "gift" her $500 a month and, once again because it is a gift, there would be no tax consequences. For her, it would be like receiving a 6% after tax-return on her money and that would surely beat the 5% taxable return she gets from the bank now.

Remember that if the $100,000 was a loan instead of a gift, and you paid interest on that loan instead of making regular gifts to your grandmother, then she would have to report the $500 per month as interest income on her taxes. It is, therefore, essential to make this a gift instead of a loan. ●

FACT

A 1% savings over the life of a $150,000 25-year mortgage results in $53,170 less in interest charges.

GRANNY'S "FAVOURITE TAX SAVINGS & MORTGAGE HELPER" MERINGUE

1. Find out if anyone you know is able to "gift" you enough money to make it beneficial to go through this exercise.

2. When you have found someone, ensure that the amount you agree on is enough to make a significant dent in your mortgage – say, from $50,000 to $100,00 or more.

3. Arrange to give the gift giver back a regular amount that works out to less than the going mortgage rate. You can do this on installments, if you like, on generally acceptable dates like their birthday, Christmas Day, Valentine's Day and the like. After all, this is not a loan repayment schedule but rather a gift in the family tradition.

4. Keep in mind that there must be no paperwork, since the money is exchanged as gifts, not loans. The whole transaction must be based on trust, not legal documents.

"Children become adults when they stop asking their parents for an allowance and request a loan."

– ANONYMOUS

PAYBACKS ON THE BEST HOME RENOVATIONS

If you are going to renovate your home, these are the best places to get most of your money back when you sell.

% OF ORIGINAL COST RETURNED

- kitchens 68-97%
- bathrooms 64-71%
- interior painting 62-66%
- exterior painting. 62%
- finishing the basement. 50-52%
- adding a suite on the ground floor 48-50%
- landscaping. 45-49%

TASTY TAX TREATS YOU CAN'T AFFORD TO MISS

The New Simplified Canadian Tax Form

Has Only Two Lines.

1. How much money did you make last year?

2. Send it in.

THE "INTEREST COST DEDUCTION" DIP

TAX DEDUCTIBLE. Two little words that, when applied to interest costs on borrowed money, can make all the difference between an acceptable financial risk and one that eats you alive. In fact, those words can make virtually any expense more attractive. There's something alluring about knowing the government is going to pay a certain portion of the cost.

Consider these two situations: Maybe you're like tens of thousands of Canadians who own mutual funds or Canadian stocks while, at the same time, having non-deductible consumer loans that need to be paid. Or maybe you don't have outstanding loans, but you're thinking of buying a big-ticket item like a car. In the latter case, most people will go out and borrow money for the car. That means they end up paying the interest on the loan with after-tax dollars (which means for every $100 interest payment they make, they first have to earn about $165.)

Instead, what we should do in either situation, is take advantage of legislation that offers tax-deductible interest payments on loans used to invest in publicly traded Canadian companies, bonds or mutual funds. In that way, we only have to earn $100 for every $100 interest payment. The strategy is easy to implement. Simply sell your investments and then use the proceeds to retire your existing debt or to make the purchase of the car or other consumer items. Then, go to your financial institution and ask for a loan to repurchase your investments. Remember, too, that by keeping your top-quality, long-term investments with the bank as collateral, you'll be able to get a more attractive loan rate.

To understand what you've saved, all you have to do is figure out your marginal tax rate – that's precisely what you'll save by implementing this strategy. For example, if you earn between $29,500 and $60,000, your marginal tax rate is about 40%. Therefore, by exchanging non-deductible debt for tax-deductible debt, your savings on interest costs will be 40%. ●

TIP

Remember that you could trigger a capital gain or loss on any investments you sell. Of course, when you repurchase you create a new cost base.

TIP

Be sure to match the holding period for the investment you are repurchasing with the length of the loan. In other words, if you are planning to sell the investment in five years, be sure that the term of your loan is five years or shorter.

THE
"INTEREST COST DEDUCTION" DIP

1. First determine if you have any fully paid for investments outside of your RRSP, include Canada Savings Bonds, GICs, mutual funds and stocks.

2. Liquidate these holdings and use the money to pay off existing consumer debt or purchase the big-ticket item you've been shopping for. Where commissions are involved for selling the investments, be sure to negotiate a favourable rate or sell them through a discount broker.

3. Go to your financial institution and apply for a loan to repurchase your investments. Again, make sure you negotiate a favourable rate. The key to getting a better rate is to offer to bring more of your business to the bank. In addition, use the investments as collateral for the loan.

"There are only two times in a man's life when he should not speculate - when he can't afford to and when he can."

– MARK TWAIN

"MOVE YOUR DEDUCTIONS" MOUSSE

IS THERE ANYTHING more boring than someone rambling on about the dream they had the night before? I especially like the ones that make absolutely no sense but take an excruciatingly long time to tell. You know the ones: ". . . and then I was chased by my neighbour who then turned into my grade four teacher wearing a hamster head. Just before she caught me I fell into a hole and ended up in the boardroom of Apple Computers. And then everyone around me started saying, 'right R.J'."

Of course, my dreams are much more interesting than that. The other day, for instance, I dreamt it was legal to take deductions from my wife's income tax return and pool them with mine so that I got a bigger tax credit. It seemed such a beautiful way to save money.

Well, I'm happy to report, we don't have to dream about it because it's already real – and legal in some areas. For example, you have the option of moving all or some of your spouse's charitable donations onto your tax form. This can increase the tax credit dramatically. Remember that the first $200 of charitable donations produces a credit equivalent to 27% of the total donations. Subsequent donations will produce a credit between 43% and 54%, depending on the province you live in. So, if you both reported $200 worth of donations on your form, you would each receive a credit of $54. But if instead, you put all $400 on one form, the total credit could be as high as $216.

You can also transfer medical expenses to the lower-income spouse. Too often, the higher-income spouse loses the ability to claim medical expenses, because Revenue Canada's formula dictates that first you subtract the lesser of 3% of net income or $1,614 from your total expenses. The result is that there may be nothing left to deduct. By transferring the expenses to the lower-income spouse, the total medical bill increases and the number you have to subtract from that total is lowered. You can also pick the 12-month period with the highest medical expenses to further increase your total medical bill. You are not restricted to the calendar year.

One more key point to note is that age, disability and pension income credits are all transferable where one spouse does not require them to reduce his or her tax payments to zero. ●

> ## TIP
> Tuition and educational tax credits are also transferable to a supporting person such as a spouse or parent. What can be moved, however, is only the amount that the student is unable to use to reduce his or her federal tax to zero.
>
> ## TIP
> In calculating your total medical expenses, be sure to include any premiums you paid to private health plans.

"MOVE YOUR DEDUCTIONS" MOUSSE

1. Gather together all your charitable donation receipts for each spouse.

2. Total them and report the amount on the tax form of the spouse with the higher income.

3. The first $200 worth of donations receives a combined federal and provincial tax credit of 27%; additional amounts receive a credit of 43% to 54%.

4. Follow the same procedure with medical expenses for the family, taken from any consecutive 12-month period.

5. Report the total medical expenses of both spouses on the tax form of the spouse with the lower income.

"To sell something, tell a woman it's a bargain;
tell a man it's deductible."

– EARL WILSON, COLUMNIST

"TAX DEDUCTIBLE" SUMMER CAMP CRAB

WHAT TIME OF YEAR do you think married couples enjoy the most? As you'd expect, they enjoy the Christmas season, spring break and the May long weekend, but that's still not their favourite time of year. According to Richard Dawson of "Family Feud," their survey says that while a lot of people don't want to admit it, the time of the year that brings a smile to their face is that special week in the summer when the kids go happily off to camp and the parents go happily off to a peaceful home.

Those weeks become even more special when parents realize it is possible to write off some of the costs of camp against their income. In other words, Revenue Canada is helping to pay for the most peaceful week of the year. The law clearly states that for children 16 years old and under, childcare expenses are deductible from the lower-income spouse's return when both parents are either working or studying full-time. In the case of single parents who either work or study full-time, the costs can be written off not only against employment income, but also against training allowances and research grants.

This may sound too good to be true, but these are the normal guidelines that also follow for babysitting and nanny-related expenses to be written off. What is a little different is that most people do not realize that soccer, hockey and arts camps qualify as allowable expenses. After all, your children are still needing care so that you can either go to work or school. Just don't get carried away here. There are limits. For children under seven or who are physically impaired, you can write off a maximum of $150 a week; and for kids between seven and sixteen the maximum is $90 a week.

The write-off is also subject to the regular overall limits governing childcare expenses. In any year, the maximum you can write off for a child who's under seven or has a severe, prolonged mental or physical impairment is $7,000. For kids who are between seven and not yet seventeen by the end of the year, the total drops to $4,000. The good news is that for tax purposes you can use your total childcare expenses (and you do not have to itemize them for each child). If you had six children, for example, all over seven but not yet seventeen, your total childcare bill could be as high as $24,000. It wouldn't matter if most of the expense money was spent on the youngest ones. For tax purposes it could all be pooled. ●

TIP

If you are going out in the evening for business purposes, be sure to keep a record of babysitting expenses. These are 100% tax deductible as a childcare expense.

"TAX DEDUCTIBLE" SUMMER CAMP CRAB

1. Gather all the receipts you have related to childcare including expenses for sports camps and activity camps.

2. Calculate your total allowable childcare expenses and compare them to your actual expenses. Remember to include all children who were not 17 years old by December 31st of the year on your tax form.

3. If you are a couple with children, ensure it is the lower-income spouse who claims the expenses.

4. Fill out Revenue Canada form T778, which can be obtained from your district tax office.

5. Keep in mind that Revenue Canada does not trace childcare expenses to specific children, so it's the total that counts.

"When I look at my children I say to myself, 'Lillian, you should have stayed a virgin'."

– LILLIAN CARTER, MOTHER OF U.S. PRESIDENT JIMMY CARTER AND CHAMPION BEER DRINKER BILLY CARTER

"TAX-FREE BENEFIT" BUFFET

ON THE SURFACE, this may sound like one of the worst ways to reduce your income taxes. Take a pay cut. That's right. Tell your boss you want to live better and you'd like to do it by taking home a smaller pay cheque. Are you still with me? Good, because this is a great way to maintain your standard of living and lower your taxes.

Top executives use this technique regularly and there's no reason you can't too. Instead of taking more salary, they look for employer-paid perks that are not taxable. What you must understand first, however, is this strategy is only attractive if you'd be buying the perks with or without the tax break. Most of us are familiar with tax-free perks like employer-paid dental plans or educational training courses. But the list of potential tax-free benefits is far more extensive. Things like membership fees for golf or tennis clubs, for example, can be tax-free benefits to you and tax deductible to your employer as long as your employer expects to benefit from your membership. Or maybe your employer expects you to do some walking or standing on your feet – in which case he or she might cover your purchase of that pair of Rockport shoes you've been eyeing. The shoes are not a taxable benefit to you and still can be expensed by your employer. Clearly this is a much better way to receive a raise, because you don't end up having to give a huge chunk of your new wealth to the tax man.

In the shoe example, for instance, you could have received a $500 raise, paid $250 in income tax, and then used the remaining money to buy the shoes. Better, however, is to have your employer buy the shoes and then give you the equivalent of the remaining $250 in other benefits. The company's expense for tax purposes is still $500, but you now have twice the benefit and none of it shows up on your income tax.

If a raise is not in the offing, then tell your employer you'd like to take a pay cut equal to the cost of the tax-free benefit you want. That way your employer's cost still doesn't change, but your taxable income drops and you still have double the benefit. ●

TIP

Other tax-free perks you might want to consider: employer-subsidized day care, transportation to your job, subsidized meals as long as you pay a reasonable fee, discounts on any merchandise the employer makes available to every employee, uniforms and special clothing, educational costs for training if your employer can expect to benefit, and participation in a dental plan.

TIP

Whether your employer knows it or not, he or she can give you up to $100 in tax-free gifts a year. You can also receive an additional $100 worth of gifts, without any tax liability, if you're getting married that year.

"TAX-FREE BENEFIT" BUFFET

1. If you are offered or negotiating a raise, do not ask for money. Instead, ask for the equivalent dollar amount in eligible tax-free benefits.

2. Make sure that the benefits you 're asking for are services or goods that you would normally buy for yourself.

3. If you are not successful in negotiating a raise, then ask about the opportunity to substitute some of your existing salary for the same dollar amount of tax-free benefits. This will not create any additional costs to your employer, but your tax savings can be substantial.

4. See the tip below for examples of some of the tax-free benefits you could receive from your employer.

"Income tax returns are the most imaginative fiction being written today."

– HERMAN WOUK, AUTHOR

"TAXABLE BENEFIT" BAGUETTE

NOW HERE'S A CONCEPT: your employer as your personal shopper. As you know, if you've already tried the "Tax-Free Benefit Buffet" recipe, the list of benefits that your employer can provide for you and that you don't have to report on your income tax is significant. But even if the benefit doesn't qualify as non-taxable, it is still better to receive a taxable benefit and report it on your income tax than to simply buy it yourself with after-tax dollars. Again, this strategy only makes sense when it applies to items or services you would have bought anyway.

The amount you report on your income tax is equal to your employer's cost, so if your employer can get a better corporate price for something, then the advantage is even greater. Let me give you an example. By the way, if you were a fan of the Mary Tyler Moore show, you know that they regularly practised this technique. It all started when Ted wanted the television station to rent a condo for him in Hawaii. Lou thought it was a painless way to get Ted off the air, so he lobbied hard on his behalf. Ted and his wife, Georgette, went off and had a fabulous week, but at the end of the year, his T4 slip had to include an extra $700. Ted was in a 50% tax bracket, so he had to cough up an extra $350 in taxes. That still left him far ahead, because if Ted had rented the condo himself, he would have had to pay the full $700.

You can do this for virtually any item that is for your personal use. You will always be better off to have the company provide it. And other than keeping track of the transaction for tax purposes, the company does not incur any extra cost because it shows the full cost of the item as a payroll expense. You, in turn, take the full value in as income. Your savings will always equal your marginal tax rate times the full value of the item. So, if you're an average Canadian earning between $29,500 and $60,000, that means you'll save about 40% off the purchase price. For example, if an item provided by the company is $500, then the savings will be $500 times a marginal rate of 40% – or $200.

Of course, you need the cooperation of your employer to implement this strategy. If you own your own business, you can plan to do it immediately. ●

TIP

If you have been paid a commission on the sale of a product you purchased for personal use, the commission is not taxable and does not have to be reported on your income tax.

"TAXABLE BENEFIT" BAGUETTE

1. Make a list of the items that you think your employer could provide you, and that are taxable. Examples include: clothing, transportation for personal use, vacation travel or accommodation, furniture and electronic equipment. The key is to ensure the list contains only those items you were planning to purchase yourself.

2. Ask your employer to purchase these items on your behalf, and include the total cost of these as income on your T4 slip.

3. Your employer will then have to give you a raise to reflect the amount spent, or will have to substitute the cash value of the item for salary.

"The only thing standing between you and a financial disaster is your wits, and that's not my idea of adequate protection."

– FROM THE MOVIE, "BEAT THE DEVIL" 1954

THE "KID-SPLITTING" QUICHE

YOU DON'T HAVE TO TELL ME that kids are expensive. I have three and each one insists on eating everyday. The best advice I can give you is to stop looking at your children as little-eating, television-watching, clothes-buying, telephone-dominating machines. Instead, appreciate them for what they are: tax planning tools. Most financial advisors concentrate on income splitting between spouses in order to move income from the higher income earning spouse to the one in the lower tax bracket. But the same opportunities exist with your children.

This strategy applies to children under 18. That age is a significant one for more reasons than it's the year you've been praying for because they may move out and go away to college. If you give dividend or interest-bearing investments to kids under 18, all the income generated is taxed back in your hands. In other words, there is no tax advantage.

However, if you give one of your children, who is under 18, investments or cash to generate a capital gain, the return is taxed in his or her name. Unless your kid is Macauley Caulkin, chances are he or she has virtually no income, so they will be able to keep all of the gain. This is a great way to pay for some predictable child-related expenses with pre-tax dollars. For example, if you know your kids will be going to summer camp or buying hockey equipment in the future, you can give them some money for a growth-related mutual fund or stock and, years later, when the expenses come up, the kids can pay for these expenses with the capital gains they've earned. That sure beats paying for the expenses yourself. In fact, even on a thousand dollars of expenses, the savings go into the hundreds of dollars.

Now consider the alternative. If you paid for $1,000 worth of your child's expenses with the proceeds from a capital gain, you would have to cash in a good deal more. In fact, if you're in a 40% marginal tax bracket, you would first have to make $1,430 in capital gains, 75% of which would then, by law, be taxable. So, the same purchase would cost you $1,430 because you first would have to pay $430 in taxes. And, if you paid for the $1,000 item out of income instead of capital gains, you'd probably first have to earn $1,900 or more. ●

TIP
Remember that once capital gains are realized in your child's name, he or she must file a tax form even if no tax is ultimately payable.

FACT
According to a recent survey conducted for Trimark Investments, 74% of women and 66% of men are likely to have discussed financial matters with their parents.

THE "KID-SPLITTING" QUICHE

1. Give or lend your child some money to make capital gain oriented investments like good-quality common stocks or mutual funds.

2. Remember that if any of these investments pays a dividend, that income must be reported on the form of the individual who gave or lent the money to the child. For this reason, it may also be advantageous to have the spouse with the lower marginal tax rate make the gift or loan. That way, if any income must be reported back, it will be taxed at the lowest possible rate.

3. Be sure to keep a clear paper trail if the lower-income spouse is going to make the gift or loan. Keeping a cancelled cheque may be the easiest way to do this.

4. Make sure that the investments made with the money are high-quality, growth-oriented ones. Do not speculate.

5. Anticipate child-related expenses that are not tax deductible and sell a portion of your holdings to pay for them. Anticipation is key because it allows a more flexible approach to selling the investments at the most advantageous time.

"Insanity is hereditary; you can get it from your children."

– SAM LEVENSON, HUMOURIST

"YOUNG-ADULT SPLITTEROO" STEW

A FRIEND OF MINE named Barry Lavalle once told me that the most frightening phrase to a Baby Boomer is, "Mom, Dad, I'm moving back home." You'll understand this if you've spent virtually all of your children's teenage years looking forward to the time you'll have the house to yourself, only to find it filling up again. You really can't blame the kids. It's hard to pass up free room and board and all the comforts that a lifetime of mom and dad's work can bring. Well, cheer up, I might be able to make a difficult situation into a tax break for you.

Instead of letting your children nickel-and-dime you to death while at home, it might be better to transfer some of your investments to them. Now don't choke. The idea is to get the investment income taxed in their hands instead of yours. (And if they have a higher tax bracket than you do, you're the one who should be moving in with them.) The existing tax laws make this an attractive form of income splitting because, unlike doing so for children under 18, when you transfer property to young adults, the tax burden rests with them and not you. The result is that the investment income that was formerly in your name will now be taxed in your children's name because they're over 18 years old. You can either give them the money or lend it to them to make the initial investment.

I know this doesn't sound too inspiring, but it does get better. You don't have to give up the investment income. It is perfectly legal to charge your children for their living-at-home expenses, including those for food, hot water, use of the TV and anything else you want to throw in. My suggestion is that the expenses equal the amount of the investment income they receive courtesy of your gift or loan. The result is that you'll get more money from your investments than you would have if you kept them in your name, since your children's tax rate is so much lower than yours. ●

TIP

Even if your children are not living at home, you can still benefit from income splitting if you're paying for any of their expenses. Since you're likely to be giving them the money anyway, it's better to have the income taxed in their name because they have a lower marginal tax rate.

FACT

According to the latest numbers from Stats Canada, 212,000 young people between the ages of 15 and 24 left their parents' home in 1993. In the same year, another 36,000 moved back in.

"YOUNG-ADULT SPLITTEROO" STEW

1. Give or lend money to your child who is over 18 years old.

2. If you are lending the money, be sure to prepare a written agreement that states the repayment terms of the loan and the fact that it is not interest bearing.

3. Have your child invest in high-quality dividend or interest-bearing vehicles.

4. If your child is still living at home, charge him or her for room and other incidental expenses that you could verify. There is no tax consequence for doing this because, according to Revenue Canada, you are not trying to create a profit from this kind of non-arm's-length transaction.

"There's not a man in America who at one time or another hasn't had a secret desire to boot a child in the ass."

– W. C. FIELDS, ACTOR

"WEALTH TRANSFER" WAFFLES

DO YOU TRUST YOUR SPOUSE? Hey, I don't mean in that way. I mean do you trust your spouse with your money? Well, here's your chance to prove it. I've already told you about the Revenue Canada rules that prevent you from simply giving money to your spouse for investment purposes. (Actually you can do it, but all the income will be taxed back to you, so initially there's no tax advantage.)

Here's a little wrinkle to that rule that can result in tax savings for the higher income spouse. I was told this strategy by a guy I met on the bus, who knows a woman who claimed she was told it by Ivana Trump's accountant, Greg Noble. It will certainly save you some money in taxes, if your marriage lasts longer than Ivana's did. Apparently, The Donald is still mad at the accountant for suggesting it in the first place.

The attribution rules are clear that if Donald gives money to Ivana, he is taxed on any investment income earned on that money. What is not as well known is the fact that the return from the investment still rests with Ivana, the lower-income spouse. Furthermore, any income earned on that money will be taxed in her hands.

Let me show you how it was rumoured to have worked in Donald and Ivana's case. Donald gave $100,000 to Ivana to invest and a year later Ivana had earned $11,500 on the money. Because of the attribution rules, Donald had to include that income on his tax return but the money stayed in Ivana's hands. After the next year, the original $100,000 gift once again earned $11,500. Donald paid the tax and Ivana kept the money. However, Ivana also earned an additional $1,850 on the previous year's investment return of $11,500, but this income is taxed in her hands instead of Donald's. The key was that, after two years, Ivana had kept $11,500 from each year plus the $1,850 in income earned on the first $11,500 the account had made. Her grand total was $24,850. With Donald being in a 54% tax bracket and Ivana being in a 17% bracket, the tax savings were substantial. In addition, Ivana continued to gain the yearly income and the income on all of the previous years' income. At this rate, seven years later Ivana had over $100,000 in her own name, as well as the original $100,000 The Donald gave her. ●

TIP

Separating the money that has been given to the lower-income spouse, from the money that has been earned by investing that amount, makes bookkeeping for tax reasons easier. Every year it's a good idea to transfer all money, other than the original gift, into a separate account in the name of the lower-income spouse.

TIP

Remember that once you have given your lower-income spouse a gift of money, it is now his or hers despite its still being attributable to you.

"WEALTH TRANSFER" WAFFLES

1. If you are the higher-income spouse, give your lower-income spouse some money with which to make an investment. The income produced from the investment will then be taxed in your hands. Pay the tax with other money without dipping into the gifted amount or the income it generated, so that all of the investment return stays in the hands of your spouse.

2. Have your spouse reinvest that income along with the original gifted amount. The income earned on the reinvested income will now be taxed in the hands of your spouse, while the income from the gifted amount will still be taxed in your hands.

3. Once again, have your spouse reinvest all the income produced, along with the original gifted amount. All income produced from the reinvested income will now be taxable in your spouse's hands.

"I married beneath me but then again all women do."

– LADY ASTOR, POLITICIAN

"CORP-TO-CORP" CARAMEL

TRY TELLING PEOPLE at a cocktail party or the local PTA about this idea and they'll nominate you for an honourary doctorate in finance. It sounds very complicated but, in practice, it's really quite simple.

By now I've inundated you with Revenue Canada's attribution rules. They say that if you lend money to your spouse for investment purposes, the income generated will be taxed back in your hands. However, there is an exception. The law does allow one spouse's corporation to lend money to the other spouse's corporation without any of the attribution rules applying.

Obviously, in order to do do this, both spouses have to have a corporation. Don't let the idea of setting up a corporation scare you. It's easy to do, and it doesn't cost a great deal. And besides, once you do it, it will allow you to say things like, "Sorry, no can do, I have a board meeting."

The possibility of attending your high-school reunion and stating that you are the president of a corporation, should be enough incentive to consider setting one up, but the tax savings can be significant, too. Let me give you an example. Bob has a $100,000 investment portfolio that yields $10,000 a year. His marginal tax bracket is 54%, so he ends up paying $5,400 in tax to Revenue Canada. He decided to make a shareholder loan of $100,000 to his corporation, which then lent the money to his wife's corporation to invest. Her corporation's investment portfolio made $10,000 and paid $2,400 in corporate tax. The remaining $7,600 was paid out to her as a dividend. Since she had no other income, there was no tax payable. The strategy saved Bob and his wife $3,000 in taxes. ●

TIP

The spouse in the higher income-tax bracket should pay all family expenses, so the one in the lower bracket can invest his or her income.

FACT

According to author and financial commentator, Garth Turner, there will be a million-and-a-half single-parent families by the year 2016. Most of them will be headed by women, 60% of whom will be living below the poverty line.

"CORP-TO-CORP" CARAMEL

1. Establish a corporation in each spouse's name by seeing a lawyer and creating a standard corporation.

2. If you are the spouse with the higher marginal tax bracket, put money into your corporation as a shareholder loan.

3. Next, have your corporation lend the money, on an interest-free basis, to the corporation of your spouse (who has the lower marginal tax bracket.) The terms of the loan should be outlined in a signed agreement, and should specify eventual pay-back period and interest terms.

4. If you are the spouse with the lower marginal tax bracket, take the borrowed money your corporation has received from your spouse's corporation and invest it.

5. Next your corporation pays out the proceeds of the investments as dividends to you.

"It is no secret that organized crime in America takes in over forty billion dollars a year. This is quite a profitable sum especially when one considers that the Mafia spends very little for office supplies."

– WOODY ALLEN, WRITER AND FILM DIRECTOR

COMBINED FEDERAL & PROVINCIAL MARGINAL TAX RATES (%)

How many cents of the next dollar you earn will end up with the government is determined by your marginal tax rate. For example, if you live in British Columbia and make between $29,591 and $59,180, 44 cents of the next dollar you earn will go to the provincial and federal government.

1997 TAXABLE INCOME

	$6,457-29,590	$29,591-59,180	$59,181-62,195	$62,196 AND OVER
British Columbia	26.2¢	44.0¢	49.1¢	53.7¢
Alberta	25.8¢	40.1¢	44.7¢	46.1¢
Saskatchewan	29.1¢	45.5¢	50.5¢	52.0¢

1997 TAXABLE INCOME

	$6,457– 29,590	$29,591– 59,180	$59,181– 62,195	$62,196 AND OVER
Manitoba	28.4¢	44.3¢	49.0¢	50.4¢
Ontario	25.8¢	42.1¢	46.9¢	51.8¢
Quebec	38.2¢	48.9¢	51.5¢	52.9¢
New Brunswick	28.4¢	43.4¢	48.4¢	51.4¢
Nova Scotia	27.5¢	42.0¢	46.8¢	50.0¢
Prince Edward Isl.	27.6¢	42.3¢	47.1¢	53.3¢
Newfoundland	29.2¢	46.5¢	51.9¢	53.3¢

"SELF-EMPLOYED" ENTRÉES

"Business is like sex. When it's good, it's very, very good.
When it's not so good, it's still good."

– GEORGE KATONNA, ECONOMIST

"SELF-EMPLOYED" SUNDAE SUPREME

HERE'S A LITTLE BRAIN TEASER for you. What did Karl Marx, Henry Ford, Bill Gates and your grandfather all have in common? Answer: They all knew you can't get rich working for someone else. (Actually two little-known facts about Karl Marx are that he was a big Rita McNeil fan and he believed that being self-employed was the best tax shelter in Canada.)

Karl was right. Being self-employed opens up an incredible opportunity for tax planning. In fact, being self-employed or owning your own business allows you to answer one of the most important financial planning questions heard across the country: "How do I make this expenditure tax deductible?" And the more often you can figure that one out, the better off you'll be. When you work for someone else, the opportunities to arrange your affairs in a tax-advantaged way are extremely limited.

Now put your imagination on overdrive. Revenue Canada allows businesses to deduct most expenses incurred for the purpose of gaining or producing income. That's one of the main reasons that so many white-collar workers are finding it advantageous to ask their employer to lay them off and then hire them back as consultants. Others have been forced to do it because of downsizing, but in the end they have found it even more rewarding than being an employee.

But don't get carried away. There are a couple of things to be aware of before you start writing off such things like entertainment, car mileage and maintenance, equipment depreciation and travel. One of the reasons that companies are keen on letting an employee become a self-employed consultant is that they no longer have to pay benefits like medical or dental. They are also no longer on the hook for severance, Canada Pension contributions or other payroll taxes. Therefore, you definitely want to make sure you're covered in these important areas before you leave.

You also want to make sure Revenue Canada recognizes you as being self-employed and not still as an employee. The tax man doesn't care what you call yourself, as long as it's clear that you control how, where and when you do your work. It also helps if you have income from two or three different sources instead of just your former employer. As well, you should have stopped receiving employee benefits; you should be issuing invoices and receiving cheques for your work; and you should be able to prove that you provide your own supplies and can hire your own employees as you see fit. In short: act like you are your own boss. ●

TIP

It is a good idea to sign an agreement with your former company outlining all the terms of your consulting contract, including remuneration, the project's length and expectations of performance. The contract can be renewed, but it always serves as proof of your independence for Revenue Canada's purposes.

FACT

Statistics Canada estimates that there are over 2.5 million self-employed people in the country. This is the fastest-growing category of employment this decade, and the trend is gathering momentum.

"SELF-EMPLOYED" SUNDAE SUPREME

1. If you are currently working for someone, go to your employer and ask to become a contract worker instead of a salaried employee. The employer will benefit because he or she will not have to pay benefits or payroll taxes. You should also compute your cost of replacing those benefits.

2. If you are not currently employed by someone, consider structuring your affairs so that you qualify as being self-employed. Set up a business name, get a licence, print letterhead, organize a separate bank account and create a business plan.

3. Sign contracts with clients outlining the terms, payments and duration of the contracted relationship.

4. Have a plan in place to attract new customers and thus establish more than one source of revenue.

5. Keep records of all expenses you have incurred to generate revenue and conduct your business. This includes expenses related to transportation, entertainment, communication, office and employees.

"Being in your own business is working 80 hours a week so that you can avoid working 40 hours a week for someone else."

– RAMONA E.F. ARNETT, PRESIDENT RAMONA ENTERPRISES

"HOME-BASED" BAGELS

SOMEWHERE ELSE IN THIS CLASSIC, I told you about the little-known story about how Ben Cartright was able to afford the Ponderosa. Not only did he get a half point off his mortgage, but he also pioneered one of the most attractive tax-saving strategies in the country today. Imagine having Revenue Canada help pay for your home furnishings, gardener, heating bill and high-tech toys.

We should take our cue from Ben. If you're serious about creating some wonderful tax-planning ideas, then you should immediately think of turning your skills or hobby into a home-based business. You don't have to quit your day job to do it. In fact I would not recommend it. You can maintain your current position and work part-time in your own home-based business. Once you become successful enough, you can quit your job and go full-time working out of the house.

To qualify for some significant write-offs, you should first set up a specific room in your house for your home-based business. Then determine the percentage of your home's floor space that you're dedicating to doing your business, and deduct from your income that percentage of your total hydro, utilities, mortgage interest, home insurance and property taxes. For example, if you live in an 1,100 square foot condo and use 220 square feet for your business, you can deduct 20% of your rent or mortgage interest and any other costs related to the home.

This gives you a wonderful opportunity for getting creative. Because you entertain clients or prospective clients in your home, a percentage of your gardening and maintenance can be deducted. Better still, if you employ your child to do the work, you can write that off. You can then start charging them a similar amount for rent, thereby getting the money back tax-free. All the furniture and office equipment you purchase for your home-based business can also be written off, which probably explains why many people's home office is the best-decorated room in the house. And don't buy a computer for the kids. Buy one for the home office and write it off. No one will notice if the children use it once in a while.

I hope you're getting the point. Owning a home-based business gives you many options for effective planning of expenses around the home. One thing to remember, however, is that your office expenses can only be used to bring your home-based business income down to zero, though the remainder can be carried over for deductions against business income in any future year. ●

TIP

As soon as you start thinking about setting up a home-based business create a home office space and begin keeping a record of your home-related and other business expenses. Some people forget to keep records at the outset. They think it is unimportant because they are not making a profit in that year. In fact, however, these expenses can be carried forward and applied in other years against your home-based business income.

FACT

According to the Canadian Economic Observer, the February 1997 edition, three-quarters of the country's net employment since 1989 has been a result of self-employment.

"HOME-BASED" BAGELS

1. Set up one or more rooms in your home that are dedicated to your home-based business.

2. Calculate the percentage of floor space in your home that your home-based business occupies.

3. Keep records of the total home expenses for items such as insurance, hydro, water, heat, telephone, property taxes, rent or mortgage interest, and repairs or maintenance. Deduct only the percentage of mortgage interest and not any capital repayment, because you do not want to affect the tax-free status of your primary residence. (The cost of your home phone is not deductible unless you establish a separate business phone line.)

4. Using the percentage calculated in step two above, take that proportion of all of your home expenses as your write-off, but remember you can only use those expenses to reduce your home-based business's income to zero. The remaining expenses can be carried forward indefinitely.

5. To avoid any problems with Revenue Canada, ensure your home office is the principal place of doing your business. The home office must also be used to run a regular and continuous business.

"Always remember this whole thing was started by a mouse."

– WALT DISNEY

"OWNERSHIP" OMELETTE

ONE NIGHT in a swank downtown restaurant in Manhatten, I was introduced to Brent Berry, one of the junior lawyers in the divorce proceedings between Madonna and Sean Penn. I couldn't resist pumping him with a few questions. It seems that one bone of contention between the two that didn't get much play in the media was their argument about who should start up and own the small business.

I hate to admit it, but on this issue I had to side with Madonna. She was quite correct in identifying two important reasons why more benefits would accrue if she owned the business and Sean worked there. First, she realized that any new business would probably suffer losses in the first couple of years. Second, she knew that because she was in a higher tax bracket, the tax deductions associated with the start-up would be more valuable when used on her tax form.

Expenses for things like legal, accounting, advertising, salaries and office rent are first written off against the business's income and any losses can be deducted from other income. In other words, because Madonna owned the business, it provided a great way to split income. Furthermore, all the losses associated with running the business could be written off against other income she earned.

For example, when Sean opened The Bustier Barn, the business had expenses of $48,800 in the first year, including his salary. The Bustier Barn's total income was $26,500. Madonna, as the business owner, got to write off the full loss of $22,300 ($48,800 - $26,500) against other income. Sean had to file a tax form to report his salary of $20,000 and ended up paying taxes at a combined federal and provincial rate of 25%. Madonna, on the other hand, got to shift $20,000 worth of family income from her 54% tax bracket to his 25%. ●

TIP

If you project that your business will have sales in excess of $30,000, consider registering it for GST. Once it is registered you can claim the "Input Tax Credits." That means that you will be able to get a credit for any GST on goods and services you purchased for your business.

"OWNERSHIP" OMELETTE

1. If you decide to start a business, consider the advantages of having the spouse with the higher income be the owner even if the lower-income spouse is going to operate it.

2. Create a business plan including a sales and marketing plan to show your intention to be profitable. The business must have a reasonable expectation of profit but it does not have to be profitable.

3. If you start as a home-based business, apply all the regular rules about recording and reporting the home-office expenses (see the recipe, "Home-Based" Bagels.)

4. Pay a good, but reasonable, salary to the lower-income spouse for working in the business. This is an excellent way to split income.

5. Remember that all expenses related to doing the business are deductible against the revenue it generates. Any loss can then be applied to the other income of the higher-income spouse because he or she is the owner.

"A fool and his money are soon parted. What I want to know is how they got together in the first place."

– CYRIL FLETCHER, EDUCATOR

THE ULTIMATE "HOW TO GET YOUR FAMILY TAX-FREE EMPLOYMENT INCOME" SOUFFLÉ

OKAY, THE CHOICE IS AN EASY ONE: send more money to Revenue Canada because you like subsidizing Senators' haircuts, or keep it yourself to pay down debt, take a vacation or save for your children's education. We're not talking small change here. If you own your business or are considered self-employed or a commissioned salesperson, you can save thousands of dollars by getting tax-free income through some easy-to-do income splitting.

The essence of this tax-saving recipe is to take income from the highest-earning family member and transfer some of it to other family members with less — or better still, no — income. All you have to do is hire any family member you please and pay him or her a salary to perform some sort of work.

The result is that you transfer money from your hands that Revenue Canada may be taxing you at over 50%, and put it into the hands of someone who is taxed at a much lower rate. For a lot of kids this will be their only source of income. Currently, they can earn up to $6,470 a year and pay no tax.

You can hire anyone of any age, but the salary must be appropriate for the kind of work done. In other words, you can't pay your child a brain surgeon's wage to lick envelopes. Some of the common types of work performed include general secretarial duties, recordkeeping, office cleaning, and other similar odd jobs.

How significant can the tax saving be? Even if you're in the average Canadian tax bracket of 42%. In other words, if you annually make between $29,500 and $60,000 you can save a lot. Let me give you one example. Let's say your net taxable income one year was $48,000 and your combined federal and provincial income tax bill in B.C. was $14,822.67. Now, if instead, you'd employed the strategy of hiring your two children at salaries of $100 a week, you'd have ended up having a taxable income of $37,600 and a total tax bill of $10,739.63. Your total tax saving would be $4,083.04, and your kids would each make $5,200 and pay no income tax because their salaries are below the basic personal exemption. (And you thought those kids were good for nothing.) ●

TIP
Thanks to the dividend tax credit and your personal deductions, you can receive up to $23,760 in dividends and pay no tax, as long as you have no other income.

TIP
If you are a single individual with no dependents, you can earn up to $6,470 in salary and pay no tax.

FACT
When income tax was introduced in 1917 as a temporary measure, the Income Act was 14 pages long. Today, after years of simplification, it is 2,167 pages long.

THE ULTIMATE "HOW TO GET YOUR FAMILY TAX-FREE EMPLOYMENT INCOME" SOUFFLÉ

1. Decide which specific business-related jobs you are hiring family members to do.

2. Determine what a fair salary would be by industry standards.

3. Pay your family employees regularly and keep full records.

4. Make sure each family member involved files an income tax form even if he or she has no tax to pay.

5. Keep in mind that the entire relationship should be no different than it would be if you were dealing with an unrelated employee.

"The taxpayer is someone who works for the federal government but doesn't have to take a civil service exam."

– FORMER U.S. PRESIDENT RONALD REAGAN

"DON'T DROP DEAD" DANISHES

"Death is not the end;
there still remains the litigation."

– AMBROSE BIERCE, AUTHOR

"DEEMED DISPOSITION" DEVILLED EGGS

IN HIS 1953 PLAY, "The Tax Man Cometh," John Boy Walton wrote that, "As if Joe Bob's death wasn't enough, now came the tax man looking for his share of the family business. Martha, a big woman by any standard, had worked at Joe Bob's House of Hams for 21 years. And now, just when the mecca for pig meat lovers everywhere was about to be hers, Joe Bob's estate was presented with a tax bill for $32,000. She wept as she stuffed her pockets with sausage for the morning meal."

Not surprisingly, the play was never produced. Nonetheless, some of its more memorable scenes serve as a valuable reminder that an individual's capital assets (including things like mutual funds, public or private shares, the house and the cottage) are deemed to have been sold upon death. That doesn't mean they were in fact sold; it means that for tax purposes they are all deemed to have been sold at fair market value on the day on the person died. And that can create huge tax problems for survivors.

Let's say that the business of the deceased has a fair market value of $100,000 over the original cost. With today's capital gains laws, that means that $75,000 gets added to the deceased final income tax bill. That would probably be enough to push the deceased into the 50% marginal bracket, and produce a $37,500 tax bill.

There have been many instances where the tax bill created by a loved one's death has forced families to sell the family business or vacation cottage. One easy-to-use strategy employed by the rich and famous to prepare for this impending capital gains problem is to purchase enough term life insurance in the owner's name to cover the anticipated tax bill, in case of death. The cash paid out to the beneficiary from life insurance is usually not taxable. The advantage of naming the beneficiary on the policy is that the proceeds from the insurance are not subject to probate fees. The beneficiary then pays the deceased's taxes. ●

FREE

If you want to know more about insurance, the Canadian Life and Health Insurance Association has a free booklet entitled, "A Guide to Buying Life Insurance." The association's phone number is 1-800-268-8099.

"DEEMED DISPOSITION" DEVILLED EGGS

1. Make a list of all the non-RRSP or non-RRIF assets held in your name, including stocks, bonds, mutual funds, real estate and private business shares.

2. Calculate the size of the capital gains you would accrue on your total assets (outside your RRSP or RIFF) if you were to sell them now. To determine your potential tax bill, take 75% of the gain and then take 50% of that number.

3. Shop around for the best rate on a term life insurance policy that would cover the amount of your potential tax liability. Make sure the policy is automatically renewable and non-participating.

4. Name your beneficiary on the policy so that when you die the money paid out will go directly to them and bypass your estate and probate fees.

5. Have the beneficiary consider taking out the policy on you. After all, that individual is the one who will benefit from having it.

6. Remember to review your policy on a regular basis to be sure that your coverage adequately reflects any change in circumstances.

"Retirement at 65 is ridiculous.
When I was 65 I still had pimples."

– GEORGE BURNS, COMEDIAN

ESSENTIAL ESTATE INFORMATION

You look great. In fact some of your friends are telling me that you look too good but I still want you to take a half hour and answer these questions. God forbid that something happens to you so that you can't take care of your own affairs but in that case don't compound the problem with having your loved ones or the executor of your will searching for this information. Write it down and tell your spouse or other family member where to find the list.

1. Full names and addresses of surviving children and other beneficiaries.

2. Specific details of assets including:

   • bank accounts

   • GICs, term deposits or other investments held by any bank or financial institution

   • accounts with financial advisors, stock brokers, mutual funds, financial institutions or otherwise

   • insurance policies (both life and general)

- RRSP's, annuity and investment contracts

- stocks, bonds or other investments held
  (limited partnership units, an interest in any
  other form of investment)

- civic and legal description of any lands or interest
  in lands

- vehicles, boats or vessels or any other asset that may
  be registered in your name

- insurance policies for jewellery and details of any
  jewellery appraisals

- material agreements such as marital or separation
  agreements, shareholder or investment agreements.

3. Names of professional advisors including lawyer,
   accountant, financial advisor and insurance agents
   (both life and general.)

4. Provide the location of and information for previous
   years' income tax returns.

5. Accurately document your obligations, such as bank
   loans, mortgages, etc.

"MAKE YOUR WILL"
WATERCRESS SALAD

"OH, HAS HE PASSED?" "Yes, he's gone." "Kaput?" "Yeah, he's crossed over." Can you believe all the nice ways we have of saying someone is dead? I don't know why it's considered bad taste to remind people of what we all know to be true. We live and then we die. We don't know when it will happen although Bob Hope gave us a good hint about when we should start preparing for the inevitable when he said, "You know you're getting really old when the candles cost more than the cake."

We can get our hair coloured, our tummy tucked and our wrinkles laser-treated. In the end, however, we still end up holding hands with St. Peter. So why isn't everyone preparing for the inevitable?

At the risk of sounding unpleasant, I want to make sure that when you die, you don't add to the grief of your loved ones by being unprepared. This is an especially hard concept for young people to grasp, since most of them suffer from the illusion that they will live forever. But let me give you a wake-up call. Once you're married and have any dependents, it is the height of irresponsibility not to complete a will.

What's the big deal if you die without a will? Well, right off the top, you can cause a huge disruption in the financial well-being of your survivors. It is not automatic that they have access to any of your assets, including your bank account. Distribution of those assets to your beneficiaries can be delayed because there is no administrator until one is appointed by the courts. In fact, the provincial government may end up dictating who the beneficiaries of your estate are. And even worse, your estate will in all probability, end up having to pay significantly higher taxes than necessary. The list of horrors is long, but let me leave you with just one more. The court will be forced to choose a guardian for your children and that person may not be whom you would have wanted.

The bottom line is that your family needs to be protected during what is likely to be a very trying time. If done properly, a good will maximizes the proceeds of your estate and ensures they go to the people you want to receive them. It also reduces legal costs and probate fees.

I can't get a hammer big enough to hit you over the head and convince you to prepare a will now. If you already have one, I'm impressed – but when was the last time you reviewed it to ensure it reflects your current circumstances? ●

TIP
You should be aware that if you are married with no children and die without a will, after probate your estate will be distributed to your spouse. If you have a child, the first $200,000 plus one half of the remaining amount will go to your spouse and the remainder to the child. If you have two or more children, the first $200,000 plus one third of the balance will go to your spouse; the remaining two-thirds will be shared equally amoung the children. In the case of children, who are 18 or under, the official guardian may be involved in managing the disbursements as above.

"MAKE YOUR WILL"
WATERCRESS SALAD

1. Make a list of all your holdings, including property, investments and high-priced personal effects.

2. Decide to whom you want these assets to be distributed upon your death. If you have an RRSP, it should not be included in your will (you will have named a beneficiary on your form so as to avoid having it included in your estate and subject to probate fees and taxes.)

3. Choose a guardian for your children and an executor for the estate. Be sure to clear it with them first so that they know what is going on.

4. Decide what happens to your estate and children should you and your spouse happen to die at the same time.

5. Take the information to a lawyer so that a will can be drafted with clear and precise language that ensures your wishes are carried out. It is worth the $150 to $250 fee.

"Once you get over 100 you pretty much have it made. You almost never hear of anyone dying who is over 100."

– GEORGE BURNS, COMEDIAN

"THINGS TO DO BEFORE YOU'RE DEAD IN DENVER" SANDWICH

HERMAN MUNSTER. Now, that's a name that's not regularly associated with financial planning. But did you ever wonder how the head of TV's Munster family managed to maintain his unusual lifestyle in spite of the fact that he didn't work? Inherited money is one thing but I think he must have used more than his looks to prevent the government from getting too big a chunk of what his dead family members left him. Here's how he's rumoured to have set things up in order to maximize his inheritances.

Herman was a bit of an estate-planning expert. His forte was to structure his older relatives' affairs so that when they died (and left him money), their estates would not be eroded by excessive probate fees. Probate is the legal process that validates a will and probate fees are paid to the court when it provides a validation certificate. In Canada, politicians are fond of saying that we don't have inheritance taxes. True, but we do have probate fees. Any way you want to look at it, money from your estate ends up going to a government institution instead of to your beneficiaries. Herman knew a few ways to be sure the government's take from his bounty would be minimized.

First of all, Herman was an absolute stickler about making sure that when it came to RRSPs or Registered Retirement Income Funds, his relatives had designated a beneficiary (guess who?) That way, upon a realative's death, the funds in his or her plan would be transferred directly to the beneficiary's plan, bypassing the deceased's estate and incurring the need for probate fees. Second, Herman always insisted that his relatives make him the beneficiary on their life insurance policies and annuity contracts. By doing that, he again avoided getting that money tied up in the estate and incurring additional probate fees.

Herman also made sure that all his relatives held all their non-RRSP or non-RRIF assets (for example, home, cottage, mutual funds and bank accounts) as joint tenants with him. When they died, the asset, therefore, automatically passed to him, the surviving tenant.

There are many other such strategies available, such as setting up a holding company in a low probate fee province or creating a living trust. You'd be smart to contact an expert to explore all the possibilities. ●

TIP

Every province has a different formula for determining the amount to be paid in probate fees. In Alberta, for example, the rates start at $25 for the first $10,000, increasing to a maximum of $6,000 for estates in excess of $1,000,000. In Ontario, the formula is $5 per $1,000 for the first $50,000, and $15 per $1,000 for the remainder.

"THINGS TO DO BEFORE YOU'RE DEAD IN DENVER" SANDWICH

1. Be sure that you have named your spouse as beneficiary on your RRSP and RRIF plans.

2. If you have life insurance or a life annuity, phone your policy issuer and have your choice of adult to be beneficiary.

3. Put your spouse or other adult beneficiary down as the joint holder or tenant of any non-RRSP or non-RRIF assets. Start with your bank accounts and include mutual funds or stocks, real estate and bonds.

4. Consider setting up a living trust or private holding company to further escape probate fees.

5. Take your estate planning ideas to a professional to see if you overlooked anything. By coming prepared with your list of assets, a copy of your will, and other pertinent financial data, you can keep the cost of the consultation very reasonable.

"You've heard of the three ages of man: youth, middle-age, and 'you're looking wonderful'."

– FRANCIS JOSEPH SPELLMAN,
AMERICAN ROMAN CATHOLIC CARDINAL

DAVE BARRY'S HELPFUL
SELF-TEST QUESTIONNAIRE
TO SEE IF YOU HAVE ENOUGH LIFE INSURANCE

1. How much insurance do you have?

2. You need more.

3. We'll send somebody over right now.

Source: "Dave Barry Turns 40", CROWN, 1990

"MONEY-MAKING" MUNCHIES

"When investing your money the amount of return you want should depend on whether you want to eat well or to sleep well."

– J. KENFIELD MORLEY, JOURNALIST

"Financial Advisor-Finder" Fishsticks

A FRIEND OF MINE in the financial business, Rob Zurrer, was at a cocktail party at Truman Capote's house in Beverly Hills when Elizabeth Taylor came up to him. She had heard about Rob's reputation and wanted to know how she should go about choosing a financial advisor. Rob shot back immediately, "Certainly a lot more carefully than the way you choose your husbands." She turned around abruptly, grabbed a half-roasted chicken off his plate, and went off to rejoin Shelley Winters.

Rob was a little harsh, but the advice had merit. There is no sure-fire way to select the perfect person to help you with your financial circumstances, but there are several steps you can do to give yourself a good shot.

The first thing to understand is that you're not choosing someone so that you can avoid your own responsibility. A financial advisor is there to help you achieve your financial goals – not choose those goals for you. Before you start to make any financial decisions or see a professional, you should have your lifestyle and financial goals set down in a clear statement.

It is not good enough to say you want to make as much money as possible. If that's the case, buy a lottery ticket or go to Vegas. What you really have to do is get specific about your financial goals and the risks you are willing to take. You also need to produce a list of your assets, current living expenses and family circumstances. In other words, be prepared to paint a picture of where you are financially and where you want to go.

As well, before you charge off to find the perfect advisor, you should have a list of the kind of expertise you require and the type of person you're looking for. You may end up choosing more than one person: maybe an accountant for taxation, a lawyer to help you implement some of the strategies you choose to achieve those goals, and a stockbroker or financial planner to help you with your investments. If you are well prepared, with a clear understanding of your circumstances, the professional help you seek will not be expensive. Keep in mind, too, that the expense of a professional is something you'll amortize over a long period of time.

Friends and acquaintances may be able to recommend someone to you. Be prepared to interview these prospects, ask for credentials and references, before you commit to anything. In the case of investment professionals, feel free to phone the Investment Dealers Association and ask for information about the firm of your prospective advisors. The bottom line is that choosing a financial advisor is a lot like choosing any other professional such as a doctor or dentist. ●

TIP

Before you act, be sure to ask about all the related fees associated with any transaction you're thinking of making. Don't be afraid to ask the prospective professional how he or she gets paid. Is it by commission, set fee or a combination? If you are seeing a broker, accountant or lawyer for the first time, there's a good chance there will be no charge.

"FINANCIAL ADVISOR FINDER" FISHSTICKS

1. Before you seek any professional advice, put your current circumstances down in writing. Include a balance sheet of assets and liabilities, a general idea of monthly cash flow and your personal circumstances.

2. This is the hard part. Decide what your goals are both financially and personally. You must have a clear picture of where you want to with your life. The financial plan or actions you take can only make sense in this context.

3. Ask friends and acquaintances to recommend financial advisors. Be sure to ask why they are recommending them.

4. Arrange to see at least three people in the business before you decide which one to go with. When you are interviewing them, ask specifically what services they provide and what credentials they possess. Be sure you are very clear about what services you need.

5. Make sure the firm they are with is a member of the standard industry association. For example, investment firms should be members of the Investment Dealers Association or the Mutual Fund Dealers of Canada.

6. A certified financial planner or a registered financial planner should be able to refer you to other professionals when needed.

"TAKE-CONTROL" CASSEROLE

WHEN THIS BOOK WAS NEARLY COMPLETE, a dear friend of mine told me he had a recipe that should go in this book. After hearing the details about a situation he found himself in, I agreed. My friend had a stock account that had remained inactive for years with a well-known brokerage firm. Usually, those kinds of accounts are eventually passed along to newer brokers, because they have the time to try and resuscitate them.

Sure enough, my friend got a call from a broker saying that his money had not been doing much for years and would he like to consider a good stock the broker had in mind for him to buy. My friend made it very clear that he was only into long-term, no-risk investments and that he wasn't interested in being more active. The broker assured him this particular situation fit the bill, so my friend said go ahead and invest. The stock was bought in the $1.50 range. Five months later, my friend finally reviewed the investment to find it had dropped to the 6¢ mark.

My friend was down $4,500 and didn't know what to do. In my opinion, the broker did not act in accordance with the main tenet of the investment business, which is to know your client and act accordingly. There are virtually no professionals who would recommend a penny stock as being a riskless, long-term investment, yet that is what this individual broker did. Of course there are risks involved with investing, but it is a financial advisor's job to make sure that any investments he or she recommends carry an appropriate amount of risk.

I told my friend to write the brokerage house manager and apprise him of the situation. In my opinion, my friend deserved to get his money back. If he did not receive satisfaction from the manager, I suggested he then write the Investment Dealers Association and lodge a formal complaint. He should then contact a lawyer and prepare to sue.

The saving grace for my friend was the fact that his investment goals were clearly spelled out on his account form and it was obvious to any professional that the specific investment recommended did not fit the guidelines. Nevertheless, my friend wasn't entirely free from blame, either. He should have kept a close eye on his money.

The moral of this story: Just because you have a financial advisor, it doesn't mean you shouldn't monitor your investments closely. ●

TIP

No investment professional is allowed to buy or sell in your account without your specific authorization. The more specific your instructions, the less chance there is for miscommunication. If you give your investment professional permission to trade in your account on a discretionary basis, you must first sign a legal form.

"Take-Control" Casserole

1. Before you make any investment decisions, make sure you have clearly defined your goals, including the level of risk you are financially and emotionally comfortable with.

2. Ask your financial advisor specifically if the recommendation you are getting fits within your particular risk parameters.

3. Review your account on a monthly basis to be sure there's no activity that you have not authorized.

4. If you have any concern with the account, contact your broker. If you are still not satisfied, contact the branch manager in writing.

5. If you are still not satisfied, look up the Investment Dealers Association in the phone book and contact them in writing. After discussing the matter with them, you may want to seek legal advice for the purpose of suing and recovering your money.

"Choose stocks the way porcupines make love - very carefully."
– ANONYMOUS

"DOLLAR-COST AVERAGING" ASPIC

IT'S HAPPENING AGAIN. Before you can stop yourself you blurt out, "Alex, I'll take Investment Know-It-All for $500." Alex, sporting a wonderful blue, double-breasted blazer by Hardy Ames, reads, "The answer is seven years." You immediately hammer the buzzer and say, "What is the appropriate length of time to hold an equity-based mutual fund in order to remove the risk caused by market fluctuations?" "Correct!" shoots back Alex as the bell rings for Final Jeopardy. No – it wasn't the Final Jeopardy bell, it was the alarm clock. You wake up excited and slightly embarrassed for having had yet another dream about Alex Tribeck and your finances. You wonder what it all means.

Don't worry. More and more of us are having the same kind of dream in this low, interest-rate environment. We're not satisfied watching our RRSP grow by 5% or less a year and yet we're a little uncertain about taking on more risk by buying equity-based mutual funds in these volatile markets. There are two easy-to-implement techniques that can help you put your mind at rest by greatly reducing your risk.

You already know the first one, because you had it right in your dream. The risk an investment poses and the length of time you hold that investment are directly related. The longer you hold it, the more likely all the risk caused by short-term market fluctuations will be removed. And, in fact, several studies have concluded that if you hold an equity-based investment for seven years, you will remove virtually all risks associated with market movement. In short, how long you hold an investment is as important as what you invest in.

The second risk-reducing strategy is referred to as "dollar-cost averaging." The concept is straightforward. You buy equal dollar amounts of an equity mutual fund or stock at predetermined regular intervals. In other words, you might buy $300 worth of a fund on the first of every month. Over time this will average out your purchase price and protect you from falls in the market. When the market is high, you will buy fewer shares with your fixed amount; when it is low, you will get more. In this way you don't have to worry about market timing. And you will now be operating with a clearly defined plan that has a proven track record of reducing market risk. ●

FACT

The Templeton Growth Fund recently conducted an interesting test that reveals that holding an investment for the long-term mitigates the impact of poor market timing. It examined the investment history of two investors over the past 25 years. One investor always bought at the top of the market, while the other had much better timing and bought at the absolute bottom. This happened every year for 25 years. The result may surprise you. At the end of that time, the bottom-buying investor had realized an average return of 18%, while the top-buying one still realized an average return of 16.9% return.

"DOLLAR-COST AVERAGING" ASPIC

1. Choose a regular interval at which to make an investment. Every month or every quarter would be a typical period.

2. Decide how much money you are willing to commit to a specific stock or equity-based mutual fund.

3. Select a high-quality stock or mutual fund to invest in. For either case, check the long-term records of growth (10-year performance records are preferable.) Any major brokerage house would have this information.

4. Always invest the same amount of money at your chosen interval, regardless of market conditions or how you feel.

5. Commit for the long term. This is a strategy that will pay off over five years and more. Consistency is the key. Dollar-cost averaging should be a habit.

"Price is what you pay. Value is what you get."

– WARREN BUFFET, BERKSHIRE HATHAWAY

THE "40% PROFIT PAYROLL SAVINGS" PARFAIT

IT MAY SOUND TRITE, but most of us have nodded our head in agreement when someone laments that there is too much month left at the end of the money. With all of us who earn over $29,000 a year and up paying 50% of that to the government, it's little wonder there is often very little left over. The sad part of all this is that most of us can't afford to invest, yet very few of us can afford not to.

Tax burden aside, the main problem most of us have is a lack of discipline to be consistent and persistent about committing a minimum amount to a regular investment program. You have to admit it's a little peculiar that more Canadians buy lottery tickets with regularity than invest or save. I don't know about you, but at times I find it helpful to have a third party impose the discipline. Don't get excited. I'm talking about getting help with a little financial discipline.

One of the best ways to get started is to use an employee payroll deduction plan for Canada Savings Bonds. Virtually anyone can sign up at a participating office, regardless of his or her past credit history. An added bonus for young people is that it's not a bad way to start a credit history. For as little as $50 a month off your pay cheque, you can get a program going. Any interest you pay on borrowing the money to buy the savings bond is tax deductible and is, for the most part, offset by the interest you are earning.

At the end of 12 months you will own a bond outright. Now, here's the best part. You can take that bond and put it into your self-directed RRSP as a contribution in kind. It's treated the same as a cash contribution. You'll get a tax receipt for the full value plus any accrued interest. In other words, for only $50 a month you'll end up with a $600 Canada Savings Bond that, in turn, when contributed to your RRSP, will provide you with a tax refund of around $240. But there's more. Because I'm a little fanatical, I would have you take that refund and make another RRSP contribution with it. In turn, you'll get another refund for around $96 and your RRSP will now be worth at least $840. That's a 40% profit on your $50 a month deduction. ●

FACT
The maximum Canada Pension Plan monthly payout was $736.81 for 1997, while the maximum Old Age Security monthly payout was $406.34.

TIP
Shop around various trust companies before you purchase a self-directed RRSP. The fees associated with these plans vary from $25 to $150.

THE
"40% PROFIT PAYROLL SAVINGS"
PARFAIT

1. Find out if your employer has a payroll deduction plan for Canada Savings Bonds. The bonds are sold every year from mid–October until November 1.

2. Figure out how much money you can afford to have deducted monthly. The more you can afford, the better your financial future will be.

3. At the end of the 12 months, when you own the bond, go to your financial institution and establish a self-directed RRSP.

4. Transfer the bond into your RRSP and you will receive the full contribution credit for interest and the bond value.

5. When you receive your tax refund for the RRSP contribution, use it to make a new contribution to your RRSP, thereby getting a further tax reduction. You can continue to take the new tax refund and contribute it as many times as you want, up to your total contribution limit.

"The safest way to double your money is to fold it over and put it in your pocket."

– KIN HUBBARD, AMERICAN HUMOURIST

THE "SWAP 'TIL YOU DROP" SOUFFLÉ

I DON'T WANT YOU to take this the wrong way, but I really encourage a lot of people to consider swapping. Don't worry, I'm only talking about your personal finances. The reason is that far too many people have their dividend and capital gains income sitting inside their RRSP, and their Canada Savings Bonds, GICs and other interest-bearing vehicles sitting outside their plan. But you ask, "What's wrong with that?" The answer is simple. Any investment income earned inside your RRSP accrues tax free, so that the more forgiving income tax rules on dividends or capital gains don't benefit you. At the same time, the interest you earn outside your plan gets taxed to the max outside your plan. It doesn't take a commerce degree to understand that it makes much more sense to take advantage of the dividend tax credit and the capital gains reductions by putting those investments outside your plan and the interest-bearing ones inside.

But, you say, "It's too late! The damage is already done!" Well, don't worry because that's where swapping comes in. Done carefully, as outlined here, it can be a great financial strategy. It is perfectly legal to move your interest-bearing vehicles into your RRSP and then to take out the same dollar value of dividend-paying mutual funds or shares. The key is to match the same dollar amounts on the vehicles you're putting into the plan with those you're taking out.

Let's look at an example from an old CBC episode of "The Beachcombers." Nick needed to find more money to finance the remodeling of Molly's Reach. Nick had $10,000 in Canada Savings Bonds sitting in his safety deposit box, and $10,000 worth of Bell Canada shares in his RRSP. Both paid an annual return of about 4%. Nick's problem was that he was paying 40% of his savings bond interest back to the government in income tax and, at the same time, he wasn't taking advantage of the dividend tax credit because his Bell shares were in his RRSP. His net income inside his RRSP was $400 but, outside taxes took it down to $240. When Nick finally put his interest income inside his RRSP, he still made $400 but, by moving his dividend income outside his RRSP he ended up with $301 instead of the $240 he was getting before. His after-tax return increased 25% because of the swapping of investments. ●

TIP

When calculating the value of an interest-bearing vehicle to put into your RRSP, remember to include all interest that has been accrued but not yet paid out.

THE
"SWAP 'TIL YOU DROP"
SOUFFLÉ

1. Identify and add up the values of all of your interest-bearing vehicles outside your RRSP.

2. Go to the financial institution that holds your RRSP and say you want to put your interest-bearing vehicles into your RRSP in exchange for some dividend-paying stock and/or mutual funds that are currently inside the plan.

3. Make sure that the current market value of the interest-bearing vehicles you put into your RRSP is equal to or less than the market value of the mutual fund or stocks you take out. If the market value of the interest-bearing vehicles you take out of your plan are higher than the market value of the instruments you take out, then you'll have to take the difference into that year's income and pay tax on it.

4. Fill out the appropriate form provided by the financial institution that holds your RRSP. Remember that this is a direct transfer. The interest-bearing vehicles go in and the dividend and capital gains-oriented vehicles come out.

"A bargain is something you can't use at a price you can't resist."

– FRANKLIN P. JONES

THE "5% IS BETTER THAN 6% INVESTMENT RETURN" DELIGHT

HERE'S A LITTLE BIT of an investment brain teaser. When is a 5% return better than a 6% return? When the 5% is a dividend and the 6% is an interest payment. And what's the reason? Revenue Canada's tax rules. Any explanation as to why Revenue Canada has the tax rules it does is akin to asking why most men consider the TV's remote control to be a religious symbol. No one really knows. It's just better to accept that there are bigger powers at work here and adapt accordingly.

In order to get the biggest bang for your investment bucks, it is essential that you understand that it's not what you make on your investments. It's what you get to keep after Revenue Canada is through with you. The bottom line is that as far as Revenue Canada is concerned, not all investments are created equal.

The best form of investment income is dividends of Canadian corporations. Most of us would have to earn 1.35 times more interest than dividends to end up with the same amount of money in our wallets after tax. That's why a 5% dividend is worth more to you than a 6% interest payment. Capital gains are not as attractive a form of investment income as dividends from a tax perspective, but they are treated more favourably than payouts for Canada Savings Bonds, GICs and other interest-bearing vehicles.

The tax treatment of different kinds of investments carries lots of implications for your investment strategy. If you want to replace some of the income you receive from interest-bearing vehicles, you will have to invest in common or preferred shares or mutual funds that issue dividends. Dividends are not guaranteed, however, so you should restrict yourself to the highest quality companies with long-standing payout records. The good news is that preferred shares are rated according to safety of principal and the reliability of the dividend. All you have to do is tell your broker you want to restrict your investments to P1 or P2 rated preferreds. ●

AVERAGE PROVINCIAL AND FEDERAL MARGINAL TAX RATE VARIOUS TYPES OF INVESTMENT INCOME

To find out how much of every dollar you earn in investment income will go to the provincial and federal governments, find your income level on the table below. Check the type of income you will receive from the column on the left and then read the percentage. For example, if you earn between $29,591 and $59,180 and you receive a dollar in dividends, you'll pay 26¢ to the government. If you receive a dollar in interest income, you'd pay 43¢.

	INCOME LEVEL			
Type of Investment Income	$ 6,457-29,590	$29,591-59,180	$59,181-62,195	$62,196-and over
Interest Income	26%	43%	48%	52%
Dividend Income (Canadian Corporations)	7.5%	26%	33%	35%
Capital Gains	19%	32%	36%	38%

THE
"5% IS BETTER THAN 6% INVESTMENT RETURN"
DELIGHT

1. Check with your financial advisor about high-quality, dividend-oriented mutual funds, P1 or P2 rated preferred shares, or blue chip common shares with perfect dividend payout records.

2. Check the dividend rates of these against the interest you are currently getting in your GICs, Canada Savings Bonds, savings account, or other interest-bearing vehicles.

3. As a rule-of-thumb, if the interest payouts are not 1.35 times bigger than the dividends you could get, consider switching some of the interest-bearing vehicles into dividend-paying ones.

"I have no use for bodyguards, but I have a very special use for two highly trained certified public accountants."

– ELVIS PRESLEY

ACTUAL RETURN ON GIC
OR TERM DEPOSIT

Advertised Rate of Return	5%
Taxes (at 40% marginal rate)	- 2%
Inflation (current)	- 2%
Real Rate of Return	1%

"RICH-DRIP" DRESSING

THERE IS A TERRIFIC scene in the classic movie, "The Graduate." Dustin Hoffman is at a cocktail party and one of his parents' friends comes up to him and, in talking about future business opportunities, says that he has just one word for him: plastics. Not bad advice, but if I had directed that scene, I would have had the family broker come up to Hoffman and say, "I have just three words for you - dividend reinvestment plan."

You can't blame me for wanting to change the scene. Plastics are so passé. However, Dividend Reinvestment Plans (or DRIPs) never go out of style. They are one of the best investment strategies available. Think about this. DRIPs allow you to buy high-quality shares at a discount, with no commissions – and better still – you don't have to put any money up. Instead of paying out their dividends in cash, many high-quality companies (for example, the Royal Bank and Wendy's International) allow you to use that dividend money to purchase more shares at a 5% discount without paying any brokerage commission.

Let's say you followed this strategy and spent $8,000 to buy 400 shares of the Royal Bank. It paid just over 4% (or $320) in dividends annually but, rather than paying that money out quarterly to you, the company used the DRIP to buy you 14 extra shares the first year. You continue to do this for years. After 10 years you would have accumulated 117 more shares and, because of superior company performance, each share would now be worth significantly more than when you first bought in. The original four hundred were now worth $52 (or $20,800), and you'd have an additional $6,084 in new shares. (In practice, the numbers may vary because of stock price fluctuations and dividend increases, but the positive investment impact is unmistakable.)

This is a great forced-savings plan that allows you to use dollar-cost averaging and take a long-term investment view at the same time. And for most of us, that is exactly what it takes to be successful. ●

TIP

When you purchase stock through a DRIP you avoid paying the regular brokerage commission (usually 2-3%.) If your DRIP also offers a 5% discount on stock purchases, your savings are significant. If the stock normally sells for $100, after commissions you would normally pay about $103. With the DRIP discount the same purchase only costs you $95. That's like getting an immediate 7% plus return on your investment.

"RICH-DRIP" DRESSING

1. Contact the Toronto Stock Exchange or any other exchange for a list of the companies that offer Dividend Reinvestment Plans and their terms. If you already deal with a full-service broker, he or she should be able to provide you with this information.

2. Invest only in stocks that you want to own long term. Choose the one you want and, if you need to further narrow your list, choose the ones whose DRIP has the most attractive terms.

3. Buy the stocks you are interested in through a full-service or discount brokerage house and have them registered in your name.

4. Ask the brokerage firm you deal with for the name of the company's transfer agent or phone the company itself and ask for the Investor Relations Department. Ask the company representative for the name of the transfer agent. Contact the transfer agent and ask them to send you the necessary forms to join their company's Dividend Reinvestment Plan.

5. Fill out and return the forms and you will receive information on an ongoing basis.

"My mistake was buying stock in the company.
Now I worry about the lousy work I'm turning out."

– MARVIN TOWNSEND, CARTOONIST

"CALL OPTION" OATMEAL

"STRIKE PRICE," "strike month" and "time value" are the three phrases that could be separating you from one of my favourite ways to increase the yield on your portfolio by as much as 20% a year. This jargon is all part of selling covered call options. My friends in the brokerage industry tell me that they don't recommend this strategy because it's too difficult to explain. I agree, but the fact that something is hard to explain hasn't stopped us before. How do you explain bell-bottom pants, shag rugs, or your first husband or wife for that matter? Sure, selling covered calls is difficult to explain, but I think the information is worth it, so here goes.

Selling covered call options is a great idea if you have high-quality stocks that you're willing to hold long term but wouldn't mind selling if the price was right. When you sell a call option you're selling someone the right to buy certain shares from you. It might be easier to understand if I give you an example. Let's say you own 100 shares of Bell Canada, which you bought two years ago at $19.50 a share. Today they trade at $25. You decide to sell a covered call option, giving the buyer the right to purchase your shares at $27.50 on any business day in the next four months until April 21. In return, the call option buyer pays you $1 per share. You keep the money whether the call option buyer purchases the stock or not.

Think of it like getting a deposit for a house you're selling. You and a potential buyer decide on the price and a closing date. They then give you some money with the understanding that if they don't take the house, you keep the money.

It doesn't matter why someone is willing to buy the call option from you. They're happy to be able to participate in the price movement of the stock without putting up the cash for it. What's key here is that you get to keep the money from selling the call, whether the option is exercised at $27.50 or not. The worst that can happen is that you're forced to sell for $27.50, although you get to keep the dollar per share you took in for selling the option. On the other hand, if the option buyer doesn't buy the stock from you in the prescribed time frame, you have still added to your yield by 5% in four months. And, of course, you can then turn around and sell another call option for another time period and take in more money to further increase your yield.

When you sell call options, you are limiting your up-side potential for the period of the option in return for increasing your yield. ●

TIP

Most options are available in three-month intervals. In other words, a stock may have options available starting in January, April, July and October. The longer the time frame you give the buyer, the more they will pay you. For the longest term, ask your broker about selling special long-term options called LEAPs. These are usually one- or two-year options from which you can expect to take in 10% to 15% up front, and still collect any dividends issued until the LEAP buyer pays you for the stock.

"CALL OPTION" OATMEAL

1. Choose a high-quality stock that you are comfortable holding long term.

2. Because not all stocks have options, check with your broker to see if your stock does.

3. Open an option account with your broker for selling call options.

4. Look at the option page of your newspaper to see the available prices for selling the stock and the time frame involved. This is known as choosing a strike price and a strike month. Then check what the options are trading for at that particular selling price and time frame. For example, one call option that allows the buyer to purchase the stock at $27.50 until April will sell for $1, while another $27.50 call that expires in July might sell for $1.25. The longer the term of the option, the more money you will receive.

5. If the option buyer exercises the option and buys the stock, take the proceeds and choose another high-quality stock that you are comfortable with. If the time expires and the option is not exercised, then simply sell another one for a future time.

"When your IQ rises to 28, sell."

– PROFESSOR IRWIN COREY TO A HECKLER

"PUT" POTLUCK SURPRISE

OLE ELMER IS ONE OF THOSE little-known stars of finance who makes his living giving advice to people we know. While he refuses to discuss the details of how well this strategy worked for CHIPS star, Erik Estrada, I do know that it must have worked pretty damn well because Erik never had to work again. Maybe he did the same thing for other celebrities like Charo and Pee Wee Herman, because they never worked again either.

This strategy is a great way of getting high-quality stocks at a significant discount from their current market value. It's called *selling put options*. Simply stated, when you sell a put option you are giving someone the right to sell you a specific stock for a specific price on any day, up to an agreed-upon date. That's a mouthful, but it may be a little clearer when I give you an example.

Let's say in January you wanted to buy shares of Microsoft and found that they were trading at $110. Instead of placing an order to buy the shares, you put your money in a redeemable term deposit for four months, and sell a put option that gives someone the right to sell you Microsoft for $110 a share, any day until May. The buyer of the option pays you $7 a share for that right. Only two things can then happen. One, the option buyer can sell you the stock at $110, in which case your real cost is only $103 because you already took in $7 for selling the put. Considering you were willing to buy the stock for $110, you are obviously better off.

Not only did you take in an extra $7 a share, but you also had your money earning interest from January until May while you waited to have the stock sold to you.

The other thing that can happen to you is that the option holder chooses not to put the stock to you, in which case you keep the $7 per share. In this instance, the return on your term deposit was enhanced dramatically by the money you took in from selling the put. You can then repeat the strategy for this or any other stock. The downside is that the stock will have risen dramatically in value and you would have earned more money by owning it.

This is a conservative way to acquire high-quality stock at a reduced price. The key is to only sell put options on stock you would be comfortable owning. By the way, once you get the stock, you should consider selling call options to further enhance your return. ●

TIP

The shorter the time period for your option, the lower the premium you will receive. That is, if you give the put buyer the right to sell the stock to you for six months, you will receive more money than if you gave him or her that right for one month. You can use that fact to your advantage if the stock you are prepared to buy falls below the price that the put buyer can sell it to you for. All you have to do is buy back the put in the open market and then resell it for a longer period. Because you are extending the time, you will gain more money and give the stock more time to recover before you buy it.

"PUT"
POTLUCK SURPRISE

1. Make a list of high-quality stocks that you would like to own. Stick to solid companies with long-term growth records.

2. Check with your broker or look in the newspaper to see if options are available on those stocks.

3. Instead of purchasing the stock, sell a put option that gives the buyer the right to sell you the stock at that price for a specific period of time. For example, you may give someone the right to sell you Sun Micro Systems at $35 until April. In return, the buyer would pay you about $4 per share

4. Keep your money in a redeemable term deposit, GIC or Treasury Bill and redeem it when the put buy sells you the stock.

5. Remember that you keep the premium, regardless of whether the buyer sells you the stock or not. If you get the stock "put" to you, your purchase price is lower than you were willing to pay at the outset. If you don't get it put to you, then you keep the premium from selling the put, in addition to the interest you earned. You can then sell another put for another time period and take in more money.

"I don't care how many boats I miss.
I just don't want to catch the one that sinks me."

– CARL R. POHLAD, FORMER CHAIRMAN, MEI CORPORATION

"REGISTERED EDUCATIONAL SAVINGS PLAN" PARFAIT

I DON'T KNOW HOW she did it, but Aretha Franklin was one of the first people to predict that post-secondary educational costs would soar, making registered educational savings plans more popular. That's where the lyrics "R-E-S-P"-e-c-t, find what it means to me"came from. (I'm not sure what the "sock it to me, sock it to me, sock it to me" has got to do with it.) What's really impressive is that Aretha foresaw the positive changes that were included in the February 1997 federal budget brought to the plans.

An RESP allows you to save for your children's education without paying tax on any investment return your contribution might earn. Under the revised federal rules, you are allowed to put as much as $4,000 a year into an RESP, up to a 21-year maximum of $42,000 per named beneficiary of the plan. I prefer the idea of a Family Registered Educational Savings Plan, because it allows for more than one beneficiary. This means you can put all your children under one plan. The contribution limits are per beneficiary, so if you have two kids, you can put in as much as $8,000 a year, to a final maximum of $84,000. A further advantage of this plan is that if one of your children decides not to attend a post-secondary institution, you do not have to deregister the plan. The second beneficiary qualifies to use all the funds.

The difference between a contribution to an RESP and one to an RRSP is that you don't get a tax deduction for your RESP contribution. The good news, however, is that when you take the contribution portion out of the RESP, it is not taxed. For both plans, once the money's inside, it grows tax free. The proceeds of the RESP must be used by the beneficiary to attend, full-time, an approved post-secondary educational institution in an approved program.

There are numerous RESPs around, so shop carefully. I recommend the self-directed plans because they let you invest in a variety of mutual funds, stocks and bonds. These plans are offered by major brokerage firms and other financial institutions. Be sure to check the set-up fees and ongoing administration fees, much in the same way you would for an RRSP. If you have any questions most financial institutions have free brochures that give all the details. ●

Big Change:

The 1998 federal budget made RESPs more attractive by giving a 20% government grant on contributions made for each child. The maximum annual grant is $400 for a $2,000 contribution per child.

TIP

If the beneficiary does not attend a post-secondary institution, you can take back all the contributions you made tax free. However, all of the accumulated income in the plan is taxable in your hands. If you have room to contribute to your RRSP, or if you have some carry-forward room available, you are allowed to use up to $40,000 of the income earned in the RESP to contribute to your RRSP. In other words, you first have to add the accumulated income earned on your overall income for tax purposes. Then you get to deduct the RRSP contribution. After that, any income you still have to report is taxed at your marginal tax rate and there's an additional penalty imposed by Revenue Canada of 20%.

"REGISTERED EDUCATIONAL SAVINGS PLAN" PARFAIT

1. Set up a self-directed Family Registered Educational Savings Plan for your children through a national brokerage firm or other financial organization that offers a wide array of investment options.

2. Contribute to the plan yearly, if your circumstances allow, up to a maximum of $4,000 per child per year. The total contribution you can put in over a 21-year period is $42,000 per child. You do not have to contribute yearly.

3. Keep in mind that, to use the RESP funds, the beneficiary must attend a qualified post-secondary level course for at least 10 hours a week for three consecutive weeks at a qualifying institution. If the college or university is out of the country, then the course must run for at least 13 consecutive weeks.

4. Consider investing the plan's funds in a variety of instruments, including mutual funds, stocks, bonds and money market instruments. Unlike RRSPs, there is no foreign content restrictions on RESPs, so the funds could be 100% invested in foreign securities.

5. Note that the plan must be deregistered within 25 years if the funds in it have not been used by the beneficiary for post-secondary education.

"Money is the only substance which can keep the world from nicknaming a citizen 'Hey, you!'."

– WILSON MIZNER, AUTHOR

THE RULE OF 72

How long will it take to double you're money? That's easy, simply divide the rate of return you're getting into 72. For example, if you're getting 10%, divide that into 72 to come up with 7.2 years.

RATE OF RETURN	YEARS REQUIRED TO DOUBLE INVESTMENT
4%	18
5%	14.4
6%	12
7%	10.3
8%	9
9%	8
10%	7.2
11%	6.5
12%	6

"SECURITY" SMORGASBORD

"The question isn't at what age I want to retire,

it's at what income."

– GEORGE FOREMAN, PROFESSIONAL BOXER

HOW MANY PAY CHEQUES DO YOU HAVE LEFT UNTIL RETIREMENT?

AGE	YEARS BEFORE RETIREMENT	NUMBER OF CHEQUES
25	40	960
30	35	840
35	30	720
40	25	600
45	20	480
50	15	360
55	10	240

THE APPLE PIE OF FINANCE

I FEEL A LITTLE BIT LIKE Elizabeth Taylor's twenty-third husband, George Clooney, when he said on their wedding night, "I know what to do. I just don't know how to make it interesting." (Okay, so maybe it wasn't George Clooney but it was one of those Hollywood hunks.) I'm going to suggest you go down the most-beaten track in the history of Canadian finance.

I am talking about Registered Retirement Savings Plans. The reason you constantly get told to invest in an RRSP is that, for most of us, it's an excellent idea. By nature it's a long-term investment that helps to alleviate any risk you might assume in your other investment. And – probably the main reason that most people buy RRSPs – it lets you get an immediate tax break.

One of the most disconcerting financial statistics we hear every year is that only about 35-50% of those people eligible to make an RRSP contribution actually do. And of those who do, only 15% contribute the maximum they're allowed to. How bright is that. We wrestle with each other every year to save 50% on hundreds of items on Boxing Day. But when it comes to taking advantage of a 40-54% return on our investment dollars (thanks to tax breaks) the majority of us pass it up.

You have to wonder about the financial wisdom of saying "no" to getting a guaranteed $1,000 investment for as little as $460. But that's exactly what contributing to an RRSP does. It's like buying your investments at a discount.

It's like having Revenue Canada pay for part of your investment portfolio. It's like getting the best guaranteed investment return in the world.

There is no shortage of free information outlining your contribution limits and all the details associated with setting up an RRSP. Any financial institution can explain them to you. My purpose here is to shake you by your lapels and plead with you not to let this great opportunity pass you by. There is no better deal in the country. ●

TIP
The most popular investments for self-directed RRSPs include Canada Savings Bonds, Treasury Bills, mutual funds, certain small business shares, and shares of stocks listed on Canadian and American stock markets.

FACT
According to a recent survey, conducted by AC Neilsen, four out of five people aged 18 to 35 have no retirement plan.

THE APPLE PIE OF FINANCE

1. Look in the blue pages of the phone book under "Government of Canada" and find the number for Revenue Canada. Call and ask what your RRSP contribution limit is. This also appears on your previous year's tax assessment.

2. Decide what kind of RRSP investments are right for you according to the risk you're willing to take. Typical investment choices will be those that offer long-term growth (such as mutual funds and blue chip stocks) and strictly guaranteed investments (such as GICs, term deposits and Canada Savings Bonds.)

3. Shop around to compare administration fees and guaranteed rates of returns.

4. Choose the financial institution you want to hold your RRSP, go and fill out the necessary forms and make your cash contribution to the plan. You can also make a contribution in kind by placing Canadian mutual funds, stocks or bonds in your plan. The market value on the day you put them in is used to compute the value of your contribution.

5. If you have any questions about RRSPs, visit any financial institution. They all have free booklets on the subject, available to anyone.

"I'm living so far beyond my income that we may almost be said to be living apart."

– e. e. cummings, POET.

THE "PAY-OFF, PAY-IN NOW" PAELLA

ONE OF THE NICEST GUYS I've met in the financial business is David Chilton, author of *The Wealthy Barber*. David is also a wonderful speaker on financial matters. I had a chance to talk with him after he had just completed a series of seminars around the country. I asked him what would be his most important piece of advice if he could tell someone just one thing. He reflected for a moment and said, with only a hint of a smile, "Buy *The Wealthy Barber*." (He hadn't seen this book yet.)

I said, "No, seriously, Dave. What is the biggest mistake you see people making?" He laughed and said he was serious – but then added that procrastination is by far the biggest mistake people make. I agree. It is also the most expensive.

Whether you delay paying off non-deductible consumer loans or put off making RRSP contributions, procrastination will kill you. Compounding your debts will kill you. The flip side, compounding your investment returns, will make you rich. Yet it doesn't seem to matter how many times we hear that message; most of us still manage to put off making the right moves indefinitely.

If I haven't already convinced elsewhere in this book, let me give you another example of why starting your RRSP early can make a monstrous difference in your net worth. Do you remember TV's Dr. Douggie Howser and his friend Vinnie? Both knew all about starting their RRSPs early, but Douggie did something about it and Vinnie didn't. Douggie started investing $2,000 a year from the age of 21 until he turned 27. The show was cancelled and he never contributed again. Vinnie, meanwhile, finally got a job after the show's cancellation, set up his own RRSP at age 27, and contributed $2,000 every year for the next 38 years. In both cases the plans received a 12% return. By the time the two child stars turned 65, Douggie's $12,000 contribution (made over six years) had turned into $1,348,440, Vinnie's $76,000 contribution (made over 38 years) had turned into $1,366,020. The difference was a mere $17,580. No wonder all the viewers thought Douggie was a genius. ●

TIP

If you had bought any reputable North American equity mutual fund at the very top of the market in any of the last 20 years, and then sold it at the bottom of the market five years later, you would still have made a significant return on your money. More proof that the length of time you hold an investment is more important than your selection of the investment itself.

THE "PAY-OFF, PAY-IN NOW" PAELLA

1. Get committed to taking action immediately, first to pay off your consumer debts and second to begin some serious investing.

2. Make a list of your current debts, focus on those at a high-interest rate debt.

3. Commit to paying off your high-interest rate debt like department store credit cards, as well as, your VISA® and MasterCard®, by taking a lower-rate consumer loan from a financial institution, and then pay the loan off monthly. Do not use your credit cards again until you have paid that debt off.

4. Set up an RRSP immediately with the financial institution of your choice.

5. Create a plan to start making consistent contributions to your RRSP. You might consider getting involved with a forced savings plan (such as a payroll savings plan with Canada Savings Bonds or taking out an RRSP loan that you pay off monthly.) Some mutual funds also can arrange monthly contributions.

"Tomorrow is the busiest day of the week."

– SPANISH PROVERB

THE LOW CAL "BIG MONEY" STARTER

THIS IS ONE OF THOSE little techniques that can make make a lot of money, but no one seems to find the time to do it. Let me ask you: Who's the most important person in your life financially? Who do you give the most money to? Is it your spouse? Your kids? No, of course not. Your biggest partner in virtually every financial endeavour is the government. For any of us lucky enough to earn over $29,000 a year, chances are that for every new dollar we generate in income or through investments, half of it will go to some level of government. That's why any time we can avoid the tax grab, we should.

As I mentioned earlier, the best place to start reducing the tax bite is through RRSPs. Of course most Canadians appreciate this, but they still don't take maximum advantage of it. Even those of us who make yearly contributions usually don't get the biggest bang for our buck. We shop around for the best investment return, yet ignore some of the easiest money available. Unbelievably, we turn our noses up at tens of thousands of dollars over the life of our RRSP.

"But how can this be?" you ask. "What have I been doing wrong?" The answer is simple. All you need to do is start making your contribution at the beginning of the year instead of at the last minute, in the last week of February in the following year. Even if you don't start contributing at the beginning of the year until you're 40, the difference can be substantial by age 65. Here's an example. Let's say you achieve an annual return on your RRSP of 10%. If, starting at age 40, you were to make an annual $3,000 contribution at the beginning of each year instead of the end, you would have an extra $32,500 by the time you hit 65.

The extra earnings get into hundreds of thousands of dollars when you make maximum contributions over longer periods of time. The point is that most of us are passing up tons of money needlessly. Even if you can't afford to make the lump sum payment in January, you would still earn tens of thousands of extra dollars by making monthly contributions. As Bo Jackson once said for Nike, "Just do it." ●

TIP

If you started at age 30 contributing $3,600 to an RRSP at the beginning of each year and continued doing so until you're 65, you will earn (based on an average annual return of 10%) more than $97,000 than if you always contribute at the deadline.

FACT

According to a recent survey, conducted by AC Neilsen, 25% of adult Canadians have not put a single dollar aside for retirement. Of that group, nearly half stated that "lack of money" was the reason for failing to put money aside for retirement.

THE LOW CAL "BIG MONEY" STARTER

1. Make your RRSP contribution at the beginning of the year instead of 14 months later at the March 1 deadline of the following year.

2. If you don't have the total amount in January, consider making monthly contributions beginning immediately. You will still be significantly better off than if you waited until the deadline.

3. Consider taking advantage of low RRSP loan rates and borrow the money so that you can contribute at the beginning of the year. The money you earn in the RRSP will offset any loan charges. It also creates a good forced savings plan.

"If only God would give me a clear sign. Like making a large deposit in my name in a Swiss bank."

– WOODY ALLEN

HOW BIG A NEST EGG DO YOU NEED TO PRODUCE RETIREMENT INCOME?

(your savings earn 8%)

TO PRODUCE RETIREMENT INCOME OF	YOU NEED A SAVINGS OF
$20,000	$250,000
$25,000	$312,500
$30,000	$375,000
$35,000	$437,500
$40,000	$500,000
$45,000	$562,500
$50,000	$625,000

THE "DIRECT CONTRIBUTION" POWER AID

HERE'S A PIECE OF ADVICE that will raise a few eyebrows: continue working your tail off, but don't accept that bonus from your company and, if you can, decline a pay cheque or two. Or alternatively skip a pay cheque. That's right, tell your boss not to issue your bonus cheque, or one or more of your pay cheques. Sounds crazy? Well it's not, and if you can afford to do this, you'll succeed in supercharging the cash in your RRSP.

The strategy is straightforward. Instead of pocketing that bonus or pay cheque, ask your employer to contribute the money directly into your RRSP. That way you'll bypass income tax, CPP and UIC deductions that would normally be taken from that cheque.

The difference can be quite dramatic to your overall RRSP. Let me give you a quick example for someone who earns between $29,500 and $60,000 a year. Let's say Marianne receives a $5,000 bonus because of her outstanding work. When she gets that cheque, just over $2,000 will have been withheld for income tax and all the other regular deductions that seem to transform any extra pay into pocket change. If she takes the money she has left and puts it into an RRSP, she'll receive a tax refund of $1,200. The result is that she will have an RRSP worth $3,000 and a tax refund.

However, if she'd had that bonus deposited directly into her RRSP in the first place, all $5,000 would have gone to work for her immediately. Her refund would equal the tax payable on the bonus, so the result is that Marianne will have an RRSP worth $5,000. In other words, she's $800 ahead by having the bonus put directly into her RRSP.

She would be even further ahead if she'd had the bonus paid into her RRSP on January 1 of the following calendar year. Then she wouldn't have had to report it as income on the current year's tax, but would have still received the full deduction (since RRSP contributions can be made until March 1 of the following year.) She would have received her tax refund before she even paid the tax due on her bonus. ●

TIP
One of the essential rules of sound financial management is "Never give the government money any earlier than you have to." That's what you're doing when you get your bonus or pay cheque paid in the next year, thereby deferring the income tax you owe for a year. It's like getting an interest-free loan from the government for a year.

THE "DIRECT CONTRIBUTION" POWER AID

1. Go to your employer and ask that your bonus cheque be deposited directly into your RRSP.

2. If you don't receive bonus cheques, ask for a portion or all of your regular pay cheque to be deposited directly into your RRSP.

3. Remind your employer that no deductions need be taken off at source for that amount.

4. Find out if your employer will defer payment of the bonus or pay cheque into the next year. That way you will not have to declare it as income this year, but will still be able to claim the RRSP deduction this year.

"The only way to cut government spending is to not give them the money in the first place."

– HOWARD JARVIS, PUBLISHER

THE "BORROW" BURGER

THIS IS ONE OF THOSE, "be-careful-you-could-lose-an-eye"strategies. That was the catch-all phrase used at our house when my mother wanted to convey that something was dangerous. (Although I must admit I still don't understand how you could lose an eye by eating too much candy.) Of course, you probably won't understand how you could lose an eye by borrowing money, but it still needs to be done carefully.

What I'd like to suggest here is that if you don't have the money to make your annual RRSP contribution, you consider getting a loan from your financial institution to do so. The reasons are straightforward. If you're an average Canadian, you'll receive 40% of the contribution back in the form of a tax refund. And the low Canadian interest rates makes borrowing a very inexpensive strategy. Keep in mind, too, that there is a great deal of competition among financial institutions to secure RRSP business. This means you shouldn't hesitate to shop around and negotiate for your loan rate. It is not unusual to get the prime rate or less. For example, the interest cost on a $5,000 RRSP loan at 5% is less than $200 a year, depending how large your monthly payments are, but the tax refund for most of us will be $2,000 or more.

The only way this could backfire is if you don't pay the loan back in a timely manner. (This is the losing-an-eye part my mother warned of.) The faster you pay the money back, the more effective the strategy. That is why I strongly recommend that you take the tax refund you get for making the contribution and pay off a chunk of your loan with it. The longer your loan is outstanding, the higher the cost of that contribution because of the mounting interest payments. Besides, you may want to repeat the strategy in the following year and you won't want the loan repayments to overlap.

One other point to remember. Because interest on your RRSP loan is not tax deductible, you're much better off borrowing money to invest from outside your RRSP where you will be allowed an interest deduction. ●

TIP

When you get your tax refund, it may prove more advantageous to pay off other consumer debt (like credit card or mortgage debt) before you tackle your RRSP loan. The reason is that consumer debt is usually at significantly higher borrowing rates than RRSP loans. And once you pay off your credit cards, do not run them up again or you'll lose the financial advantage you gained.

THE "BORROW" BURGER

1. Shop around at different financial institutions to get the lowest possible loan rate. Anything above prime is too high for an RRSP loan.

2. When you find a financial institution with a very attractive loan rate, go and apply for your RRSP loan. If you do not regularly deal there, be prepared to bring a statement of your assets, liabilities, current employment and income.

3. To get the best interest rate possible, keep the RRSP at the financial institution that gives you the loan. Many institutions will let you delay your first loan payment until your tax refund has come. If you can afford it, start the repayment immediately.

4. When you get the tax refund, apply it against your RRSP loan.

"Nowadays people can be divided into three classes - the Haves, the Have-Nots, and the Have-Not-Paid-for-What-They-Haves."

– EARL WILSON, NEWSPAPER COLUMNIST

THE "LUMP SUM" LASAGNA

IT'S NOT A BIG STRETCH to imagine that the federal government made a mistake. What's hard to believe is that they made a tax mistake in our favour.

If you're like most Canadians, you start the year committed to making your full RRSP deduction, but by the time the deadline hits, you simply don't have the money and end up making a partial contribution. The result is that each year you create what's called "unused contribution room." That's just another way of referring to the total of all the RRSP contributions you could have made but didn't. For example, if for the past five years you could have put in $5,000 but ended up putting in only $2,000, your unused contribution room would now be the accumulated total of $15,000 ($3,000 times 5.)

Which brings us to the good news. It used to be that you had only seven years to use up your RRSP contribution room or you'd lose it. However, the feds have changed the rules and now there is no specified period that forces you to use up this potentially attractive deduction until you're ready. The trouble is, too many people don't seem to be ready ever, and are losing out on a substantial amount of potential tax savings. According to Stats Can, we have about $110 billion worth of potential RRSP deductions going untapped. Since Revenue Canada can't afford to lose that tax revenue, many experts are concerned that it may change the rules again. The only sure thing is to take advantage of the situation now.

That's easy to say, but the problem is that most of us don't have the money to make a large lump sum contribution. All I can say is that the tax savings can be so dramatic, we'd all better find a way of using as much of our carry forward "room" as we can.

Many financial institutions offer special low RRSP loan rates to address this specific problem. You could also put any eligible investments into your plan, like mutual funds, Canada Savings Bonds or stocks, and receive full contribution credit for their value on the day you transferred them. If you own a business with some retained earnings, you could take some money in the form of dividends so that you could use the dividend tax credit and then make the RRSP contribution.

One more point that seems to be misunderstood is that you don't have to take the deduction on your income tax in the year you make the carry forward contribution. You can use any or all of the deduction when it is most advantageous for you. In other words, you can put your money in this year and hence guarantee that you will get to use the deduction when it suits you. ●

TIP

You can choose at any time to make a contribution to your RRSP by putting in eligible stocks, bonds or mutual funds. This is called making a "contribution in kind." Whether you're doing this to make a contribution for a single year or to eliminate your carry forward contribution room, you must remember that when you put the investments into your RRSP, they are deemed (for tax purposes) to have been sold that day. In other words, you can trigger a capital gain that must be reported on your income tax form that year.

THE "LUMP SUM" LASAGNA

1. Look in the blue pages of the phone book under "Government of Canada" and get the number for Revenue Canada.

2. Phone Revenue Canada, with your Social Insurance Number handy, and ask for the amount of your RRSP carry forward.

3. If you have the cash, put the necessary money into your RRSP and lock in the tax deduction to use in the tax year of your choice.

4. If you do not have the money, consider making a contribution in kind, using any eligible investments that sit outside your RRSP. To do this, you must have a self-directed RRSP (these can be set up at virtually any brokerage house or trust company.)

5. Alternatively, consider borrowing the money from any of the financial institutions that offer RRSP top-up loans. The rates are usually very attractive because the banks, trust companies and credit unions really want your RRSP business.

6. Use some or all of the deductions you have created on your tax form, or. decide to take some or all of the deductions in subsequent years .

"You don't see me at Vegas or at the races throwing my money around. I've got a government to support."

– BOB HOPE

THE "MORTGAGE VS. RRSP QUANDARY" QUICHE

DAVE LETTERMAN ONCE SAID that this might be the most-asked question on "The Late Show." It could well be the most-asked question on "Melrose Place." And I can count on hearing it hundreds of times during January and February. At any given time, I'm just a moment away from someone tapping me on the shoulder and asking, "Should I pay down my mortgage or invest in an RRSP?"

With today's low interest rates, handling this question becomes a lot easier. There are still many factors to consider, but for most of us the answer is to make the RRSP contribution. It doesn't end there, though. To get the best of both worlds, you should make the contribution and then use the tax refund to pay down your mortgage.

There can be exceptions to this rule, of course. For example, if your mortgage rate is at least 3% higher than the anticipated rate of return in your RRSP, you might be better off paying down your mortgage. But to make that strategy more effective, once your mortgage is paid off, you would to invest the equivalent of two-thirds of your mortgage payments into RRSPs. Fortunately, the low mortgage rates of the last few years means that this situation occurs very rarely. So my original advice still stands: contribute to your RRSP and use the refund to pay down your mortgage.

And don't overlook some of the other advantages of investing in an RRSP over paying off your mortgage. It will help you diversify away from real estate and provide you with a much more liquid investment in case you're forced to cash in quickly.

TIP

If your mortgage rate is higher than the RRSP loan rate offered by your financial institution, you would probably be better off not using your cash to make a contribution. Instead you may want to borrow for the RRSP, thereby taking advantage of the low borrowing rate, and use the cash you have to pay off some of the mortgage. When you get your tax refund, you could make an additional principal payment on your mortgage. Just make sure you pay off your RRSP loan within 12 months so that you can repeat the strategy in the following year.

THE "MORTGAGE VS. RRSP QUANDARY" QUICHE

1. Determine how much money you can contribute to your RRSP by looking at the previous year's assessment or phoning Revenue Canada (look under "Government of Canada" in the blue pages of the phone book.)

2. If your mortgage rate is more than 3% above the rate of return you expect in your RRSP, consider paying off your mortgage.

3. Make your RRSP contribution with the cash on hand.

4. When you get your tax refund, use that money to make another contribution or pay off your consumer debt with the highest interest rate. In other words, don't just blow the tax refund.

"I never attempt to make money on the stock market. I buy on the assumption that they could close the market the next day and not reopen it for five years."

– WARREN BUFFET, BERKSHIRE HATHAWAY

"FOREIGN CONTENT" FLAN

ARE YOU THE TYPE who finds a foreign accent attractive? When you choose a movie, are you drawn to something with Bridget Bardot or Sophia Loren? Oops, I'm dating myself. How about Elle MacPherson or Julia Ormond? Of course, it depends on your gender. Do you drool over Antonio Banderas or Hugh Grant? If you do, you should take that love of things foreign and apply it to your RRSP investment philosophy.

This is a variation on the theme of "don't put all your eggs in one basket." In this case the one basket is Canada, which represents only about 3% of the world's investment markets. The late 1980s rewarded those who invested in Japan; the 1990s have rewarded those who invested in America; and future gains may well lie in the developing nations of Asia. In short, there has been no time in the last 10 years when you would have maximized your returns by being wholly invested in Canada. The rewards for simply having some of your investments in other currencies were staggering. With the right moves for example, you would have made over 70% holding Japanese yen and then a further 25% holding US dollars.

Under RRSP rules, you can have up to 20% foreign content in your plan. For most of us that means buying mutual funds that invest exclusively in non-Canadian bond or stock funds. The way to do this is through a self-directed RRSP, which allows you the widest variety of investment options. This is pretty straightforward, but there is a way to even increase your RRSP's foreign content above the 20% level.

First purchase fully qualified Canadian mutual funds that also invest 20% of their holdings in foreign stocks. If you have $10,000 in your RRSP, for instance, you can invest $2,000 in foreign mutual funds. Then with the remaining $8,000, you can have Canadian funds that also have 20% foreign content, or $1,600. The result is that 36% of your RRSP will be in foreign stocks. ●

TIP
You can get an additional 20% foreign content allowance by investing in the shares of a qualified Canadian small business corporation. For every dollar invested in the shares of an eligible small business, you can increase your foreign content by $3, to a maximum of 40% foreign content. The shares in the RRSP must have cost under $25,000 or represent less than 10% of that class of shares.

"FOREIGN CONTENT"
FLAN

1. Open a self-directed RRSP. these are available through brokerage firms and trust companies. Mutual fund companies, credit unions and banks also have self-directed RRSPs that are designed for their own products exclusively.

2. Pick an international mutual fund that concentrates in blue chip equities. Review the fund's investment philosophy to be sure it is concentrated in solid growth stocks. Review its performance in each of the past five years or more. Do not rely on average returns, because they may reflect one strong year that made up for many mediocre ones.

3. Also consider the option of investing internationally by region. You could choose to be in Southeast Asian funds, emerging nations funds, or funds from any other region. Before you choose one, be sure to assess the risk component. Many of the emerging market funds can be extremely volatile as a result of market conditions and currency fluctuations.

4. There are substantial penalties levied on a monthly basis for exceeding Revenue Canada's 20% foreign content limits. Most financial institutions will keep track of this limit for you, but it's a good idea to consolidate your RRSPs to make monitoring the foreign content easier.

5. Don't forget that you are also eligible to invest in high-quality Canadian mutual funds that have a 20% foreign content.

BANANA SPLITTING YOUR INCOME

ONE OF THE STRATEGIES you'll hear a lot about when you go to happily married financial advisors is to do some form of income splitting with your spouse. A number of the recipes in this book are dedicated to moving income from the spouse with the higher income to the one with with the lower marginal tax rate – the idea being that losing 26% of your income to the tax man beats giving him 54%. You have to hand it to us financial guys – we really know our arithmetic.

One of the places that it's easiest to split income is with the help of a spousal RRSP. That's where the higher-income spouse makes contributions to a plan set up for the other spouse. Let me give you an example. Let's say Cathy Lee is in a 50% tax bracket and her husband Frank is in a 26% bracket. Cathy Lee can make a $5,000 RRSP contribution to a spousal plan set up for Frank. This allows her to write off the full $5,000 and get a $2,500 tax refund. In addition, Frank can make an RRSP contribution to his own plan. Cathy Lee's spousal contribution does not prevent him from doing this. When the money is withdrawn, it is taxed as income in Nigel's hands, as long as it has been in the plan for at least three calendar years.

This strategy is especially appropriate if it's anticipated that one spouse will have a significantly higher income upon retirement than the other. Instead of one spouse making $60,000 in retirement and paying about $19,200 in income, splitting the income evenly enables each spouse to pay only about $7,700. That's a tax savings of $3,800 every single year of retirement. ●

TIP

If the person who has the spousal plan in his or her name withdraws money before it has been in the plan for three calendar years, the withdrawal is taxed as income for the person who made the contribution. One way to shorten the holding period is to make contributions in the last week in December. That way you will get credit for that year. In other words, if you make the contribution in December 1998, you only have to leave the money in until January 2000. Your real holding period is just over 24 months, but you get credit for three years.

TIP

In the case of a marriage breakdown, the three-year calendar rule does not apply if the spousal RRSP is part of the divorce settlement. The spouse who has the plan, can take the money out of the spousal RRSP, and pay the tax personally with no repercussion for the contributing spouse.

BANANA SPLITTING YOUR INCOME

1. Estimate the total income you and your spouse will have in retirement.

2. If one spouse is projected to be in a higher-tax bracket in retirement, then go to your financial institution and fill out the forms to set up a spousal RRSP for the lower-income spouse.

3. The spouse who is projected to have the higher-retirement income should make a spousal contribution up to his or her allowable contribution limit. The spouse who made the contribution gets the tax write off.

4. The lower-income spouse can also make a separate RRSP contribution in his or her own name and receive the tax deduction.

5. You must leave the contribution in the spousal plan for three calendar years; otherwise, any withdrawal will be taxed in the hands of the higher-income spouse who made the contribution.

"When you see what some girls marry,
you realize how they must hate to work for a living."

– HELEN ROWLAND, ENGLISH AUTHOR

THE "OVER AGE SPOUSAL CONTRIBUTION" CURRY

ONE OF THE MORE INSIDIOUS TAX GRABS initiated by the federal government in this era of "no new taxes" is the reduction in RRSP maturity dates from 71 years of age to 69. The change costs you the two most profitable years in your plan; it also eliminates the final two years that you could make a contribution and get the deduction; and it forces you to collapse the plan no later than December 31 of the year you turned 69 which, in turn, means you'll start paying tax on the proceeds of your plan two years earlier.

Some strategies do exist that can help you alleviate the tax bite created by the collapse of the plan, but it is difficult to figure out a way to still make the contributions and get the deductions. Difficult, but not impossible.

There is one little loophole you could use, provided your spouse has not yet turned 69. Nothing in the law prevents you from continuing to make spousal contributions until and including the year he or she turns 69. It doesn't matter that you're not eligible for an RRSP yourself; you can still make the contribution and get the deduction in a spousal RRSP.

In fact this strategy can be taken even one step further if you care to contemplate it. Forgive me for making the suggestion, but if you happen to pass away in the year when your spouse is still 69 or younger, the executer of your will can use some of your assets to make one last spousal contribution. Now this may seem like financial planning in the extreme, but why not have the satisfaction of cheating the tax man out of a few last dollars? Since your estate must file a final tax return, it only makes sense to include the deduction for your spousal contribution. (This last deduction may prove very valuable considering that your death can trigger the deemed sale of your investment assets and create a tax liability.) ●

Tip

The fact that you made a spousal contribution does not prevent your spouse from still making a full allowable contribution in his or her own plan in the same year. In other words, your spouse can contribute up to 18% of his or her earned income into an RRSP at the same time you're contributing to the spousal plan.

Fact

In Garth Turner's book, entitled *The Strategy*, he states that by 2017 almost 40% of the entire Canadian population will be over 50. He also goes on to say that the average Baby Boomer will spend 30 years in retirement. Turner estimates that each of us will need between $800,000 to $1,000,000 in savings to live comfortably in retirement.

THE "OVER AGE SPOUSAL CONTRIBUTION" CURRY

1. Go to any financial institution and set up a spousal RRSP.

2. Regardless of your age, continue to make spousal contributions up to and including the year your spouse turns 69.

3. Make sure you take the spousal RRSP contribution as a deduction off your taxes.

4. Ensure your will includes clear instructions to have your estate make one final spousal contribution. The final deduction will be taken off the income tax form that your estate files in the year of your death.

*"All work and no play makes Jack a dull boy
— and Jill a rich widow."*

– EVAN ESAR, AUTHOR

"DEATH BY TAXES" TORTE

I HOPE THIS DOESN'T COME AS A SURPRISE but the truth is you aren't going to live forever. Even Mel Gibson packed it in after an extra 40 years in his not-so-classic movie "Forever Young." Don't get me wrong, you look great but that shouldn't stop you from planning for the inevitable. And by that I mean making a simple phone call which will ensure that the happiest person once you're gone is not the tax man.

What a tragedy it would be if, after enduring and even implementing all the RRSP advice you've been bombarded with over the years, you forget doing the one little thing that can prevent Revenue Canada from confiscating half your RRSP when you die. "What?" you claim. "That can't be right. As if being dead weren't bad enough. . . ." Unfortunately, you have to remember that when you die, you're deemed to have sold or cashed in all your assets. This, of course, is bad news for your RRSP. The entire value of your plan is deemed to have been cashed in on that day and the amount gets added to your income on your final tax return. That's enough to put virtually all of us in a 50%-plus tax bracket and cost us half our RRSP.

There is, however, an easy way to avoid having your RRSP included in your estate. All you have to do is be sure to designate your spouse as your beneficiary on your RRSP form. If you haven't done that yet, simply drop a note to the institution that holds your RRSP, stating who your beneficiary is. If your spouse is under 69, the RRSP proceeds can be transferred directly into their RRSP. If, on your death, your spouse is over 69 then the proceeds can be transferred to a Registered Retirement Income Fund, life annuity or term annuity.

The point is that your spouse does not have to pay any tax on the transferred RRSP assets until they are taken from his or her plan. By the way, are you a Seinfeld fan? Haven't you ever wondered where George Castanza gets the money to live on? The answer is simple, but even the most ardent fans aren't aware that when George's fiancée, Susan, passed away, he was the beneficiary on her RRSPs. He now takes out the money on a quarterly basis. ●

TIP

As I told you earlier in the book, interest on your RRSP loan is not tax deductible. It is much better to make your contribution with any cash on hand, and borrow money to invest outside your RRSP because you'll be allowed an interest deduction. Too many of us do it the other way around – we borrow for our RRSP contribution and pay cash for our investments outside.

FACT

According to Stats Canada, Canadians are living longer than ever before. The average life expectancy for males is 74.61 years; for females it is 81 years.

"DEATH BY TAXES" TORTE

1. Ensure that when you open an RRSP, you include the name of your beneficiary on the form.

2. If you already have an RRSP, contact your financial institution and make sure you have a beneficiary named on the form.

3. If you do not have a beneficiary designated, send the financial institution the request in writing, stating who your beneficiary is. Keep a copy of the letter and ask for written confirmation.

"A sure sign of old age is when you hear 'snap, crackle, and pop' and it isn't your breakfast cereal."

– ROBERT ORBEN, HUMOURIST

GET A 75% RETURN ON YOUR RRSP CONTRIBUTION INSTANTLY

- original contribution $2,372.00
- 43% marginal tax bracket
- all tax savings reinvested

ANNUAL RRSP INVESTEMENT	TAX SAVINGS REINVESTED
$2,372.00	$1,020.00
1,020.00	439.00
189.00	81.00
35.00	15.00
15.00	6.00
6.00	2.00
3.00	1.00
Totals $4,160.00	$1,788.00

Original Contribution $2,372.00
Total Tax Savings . . . .+ 1,788.00
Total RRSP Value $4,160.00

How To Be A Millionaire – Guaranteed!

If you want to be a millionaire, this is how much you would have to invest in your RRSP at 10%, starting at different ages to end up with a million dollars at age 65.

Starting at	Invest
25 years old	$22,095
35 years old	$57,300
45 years old	$148,600

MAKING SENSE OF ABBREVIATIONS

CPP .... Canada Pension Plan

CSB .... Canada Savings Bonds

DRIP ...... Dividend Reinvestment Plan

GAA .... Goals Against Average (not used in the book but useful for comparing goalies)

GIC .... Guaranteed Investment Certificate

GST .... Goods and Services Tax

LEAP .... Long-Term Equity Anticipation Securities

NCD .... No-Can-Do, (not specifically mentioned in the book, but a very good response to have ready when asked to do household chores)

PST .... Provincial Sales Tax

RBI .... Runs Batted In (not used in the book, but I thought you should know)

RESP .... Registered Educational Savings Plan

RRIF .... Registered Retirement Income Fund

RRSP ...... Registered Retirement Savings Plan

Stats Can .. Statistics Canada

UIC .... Unemployment Insurance Contributions (now called EI or Employment Insurance)

ABOUT THE AUTHOR

Michael Campbell is a dead ringer for a young Robert Redford. He is six foot three, and 195 lbs. of rippled flesh. (Oh, we forgot, there's a picture on the cover.) Okay, so maybe that's being a little optimistic.

Michael may not be a dead ringer for Redford, but he is one of the best-known financial commentators in the country. He has been the business analyst for BCTV news and the national Canada Tonight broadcast. He is currently the host of Western Canada's most popular financial radio show. "MoneyTalks" is heard from Victoria to Toronto on the WIC radio network. He is also the business columnist for the Vancouver Sun.

His background includes working nine years in the investment business and he continues to be a regular lecturer on economic and financial matters. He is the owner of three successful businesses. Michael lives in West Vancouver with his wife, Cathy, daughter, Courtney, and sons, Charles and William. ●

You Can Hear Michael Campbell's "Money Talks" On The Following Radio Stations

All Broadcast Saturday Morning
from 8:30 am - 10:00am

Vancouver - CKNW
Victoria - C-FAX
Parksville/Qualicum
Kamloops - CHNL
Merritt - CJNL
Ashcroft/Cache Creek - CINL
Clearwater - CHNL -1
Penticton - CKOR
Oliver - CJOR-1
Chilliwack - CHWK
Penticton - CKOR
Summerland/Peachland - CHOR
Princeton - CIOR
Hope - CKGO

All Broadcast Saturday Morning
Saturdays from 9:30am - 11:00am

Calgary - CHQR
Edmonton - CHED

Saturdays from 10:30 am to 12:30 pm

Winnipeg - CJOB

Saturday from 11:30 am to 1:00pm

Kitchener - CKGL

Money Talks can also be heard Saturdays on the internet from 8:30am - 11:00am
Pacific Time at **www.cknw.ca**

Visit the Money Talks Web Site at www.moneytalks.net